ART AS ACTIVIST

Published on the occasion of an exhibition organized from the collections
of the Moravian Gallery, Brno, Czechoslovakia, and developed for circulation
by the Smithsonian Institution Traveling Exhibition Service.
Marta Sylvestrová and Dana Bartelt, curators.

ART AS ACTIVIST

REVOLUTIONARY POSTERS FROM CENTRAL AND EASTERN EUROPE

SMITHSONIAN INSTITUTION TRAVELING EXHIBITION SERVICE

in association with
UNIVERSE PUBLISHING

Published in the United States of America in 1992
by UNIVERSE
300 Park Avenue South
New York, NY 10010

92 93 94 95 / 10 9 8 7 6 5 4 3 2 1

Art as activist: revolutionary posters from Central and Eastern Europe.
     p. cm.
     Includes index.
     ISBN 0-87663-623-7
     1. Europe, Eastern—Politics and government—1945—Posters. 2. Political
posters. I. Smithsonian Institution.
DJK50.A78 1992
741.6'74'0943074—dc20   91-14849
          CIP

Printed in Singapore

Frontispiece:
Untitled, *Vilnis Piķis, Latvia,1988, gouache.*
Piķis expresses his wish for freedom from the Soviets by depicting the morning star, a symbol
of independent Latvia, blazing through the Kremlin wall.

Acknowledgments of permission to reprint copyrighted material appear on page 160.

CONTENTS

In Front of the Mirror
Ferenc Baráth
Yugoslavia, 1986

In this poster, Baráth substitutes a pen for a hammer, suggesting the pen is more powerful than force.

ACKNOWLEDGMENTS

The exhibition and book for *Art as Activist* began to take shape as Berliners dismantled the Wall and Czechoslovak voters elected a dissident playwright president. As exhibition research progressed, television captured a startled Ceaușescu gazing out at throngs of outraged demonstrators in Bucharest. Democratic elections were changing the face of government in Hungary, Bulgaria, and Poland. Now, as *Art as Activist* nears completion, the independent Baltic republics are striking uneasy alliances with the Soviet Union, whose very existence remains uncertain.

Human energy fueled these sweeping changes. In the posters created during the frenzied revolutions of Central and Eastern Europe, one sees an explosion of free expression and political passion that the media only fleetingly captured. When this exhibition was being prepared, however, information and insights could only be provided by artists, writers, and curators who were themselves at the forefront of underground, revolutionary events.

One such person, Dr. Marta Sylvestrová of the Moravian Gallery in Brno, Czechoslovakia, was actively collecting posters as mass public demonstrations were just beginning. Long before other museum curators recognized the importance of poster images in documenting the revolutions of 1989 and '90, she had already established close contact with graphic artists and writers, many of whom had spent a lifetime as dissidents. In the process she amassed what today is a renowned collection of contemporary poster graphics that brought extraordinary talent out of obscurity. Dr. Sylvestrová's curatorial imprint is represented in this book, but her administrative contributions to *Art as Activist,* while less visible, were equally profound. At a time when even the most basic support functions of international loan exhibitions—cultural ministry assistance, telephone and cable services, postal operations, official translators—were in a state of flux, she succeeded in locating museum-quality graphics as well as carrying out complicated loan negotiations, studio photography, and transatlantic art shipments.

No Central European curator in the late 1980s could have embarked independently on an exhibition like *Art as Activist* without support from a trusted colleague in the West. For Dr. Sylvestrová, that person was Dana Bartelt, a North Carolina-based graphic artist and college art instructor, who in 1989 agreed to serve from afar as the exhibition's co-curator. Ms. Bartelt's artistic talent, as well as her extensive personal knowledge of contemporary graphics in Central and Eastern Europe, strengthened beyond measure the design of this book, and the scope and visual boldness of *Art as Activist.* But these contributions alone do not acknowledge the role she played in translating the aspirations of her Czech colleague into an exhibition project tailored to the American public. Ms. Bartelt wrote the original project proposal that brought *Art as Activist* to the Smithsonian, designed catalog mock-ups, reviewed exhibition scripts, and routinely traveled to Czechoslovakia to assist Dr. Sylvestrová firsthand. Her tenacity, and her commitment to the long-disenfranchised community of graphic artists in Central and Eastern Europe, ensured from the beginning that *Art as Activist* would become a reality.

Alongside the revolutionary posters, *Art as Activist* includes equally passionate artistic and political statements in the form of short essays, poems, and quotations. A great number of the literary works in this book were selected by Michael March, editor of *Child of Europe,* a recent anthology of Eastern European poetry, and founder of the Eastern European Forum at the Institute of Contemporary Arts in London. Mr. March shared with us not only his talent, but his invaluable knowledge of Central and Eastern European writing.

The poster images in *Art as Activist* chronicle fast-paced, complex political events. The roots of these events go as far back as the First World War, encompassing the whole of Europe and beyond. Given the enormous range of subject matter that needed to be summarized for this project, we are indebted to Gale Stokes of Rice University, Sally Hoffmann from the Smithsonian Institution, Maria Latynski and Christian Hunter from the Woodrow Wilson Center, Gilbert Smith of North Carolina State University, and the Eastern European division of the Library of Congress. These historians and researchers encapsulated seventy years of world history, as well as shifting political currents that characterize Central and Eastern Europe today, in clear and compelling texts.

Many aspects of public exhibitions involve work that public audiences in fact never see. Yet often the invisible functions of museum programs determine the success of the final product. *Art as Activist* benefitted from the the time and talents of individuals from Washington to Warsaw, Brno to Budapest. Although the tasks and details that each person handled are too numerous to recount here, we extend special thanks to these individuals, without whom this exhibition and publication would not be taking place. From the Moravian Gallery: Director Jaroslav Kačer, K. Holešovský, head of the department of applied arts, and Miroslava Pluhačková. For their assistance in gathering materials: Alf and Bea Buckert, directors of Studio 13 in Berlin-Lichtenberg; Katalin Bakos, poster collection curator, Hungarian National Gallery, Budapest; Joanna Fabisiak, University of Warsaw; Janina Fialkovska, director of the Poster Museum, Wilanów, Poland; Petr Oslzlý of the President's Office, Prague Castle; and Zdzislav Schubert, poster collection curator, National Museum Poznań. Also, John Berta, Boris Bućan, Manfred Butzmann, Juazos Galkus, Bissy Genova, Konstantin Geraymovich, Nick and Karla Hammer, Mary Haskell, Andrei Kolosov, Valeria Kovrigina, Ivo Lahoda, Lyuba Lukova, Gunárs Lusis, Piotr Młodożienec, Maria Rus, Martina Sylvestrová, Zdeněk Ziegler, and Klara Zieglerova.

This project was blessed by the arrival in Washington in 1990 of Jiří Šetlik, an art historian and revolutionary turned diplomat, Cultural Counselor at the Embassy of the Czech and Slovak Federal Republic. Mr. Šetlik's critical summation of the history of the poster was a guiding principle to the book. We are grateful for the assistance of Czech Minister of Culture Milan Uhde and Jindrich Kabat.

We are indebted to the staff of the Office of Exhibits Central for their keen eye to detail in the development of the script and the design and production of the exhibition: Pat Burke, Diana Cohen, Karen Fort, Eve MacIntyre, Walter Sorrell, and Ruth Trevarrow. Also thanks to conservators Tim Vitale and Antoinette Dwan. Many members of SITES staff contributed their efforts to the myriad administrative, registrarial, and program activities that *Art as Activist* generated: Frederica Adelman, Kelli Roberts Brya, Ken Fenty, Liz Hill, Marie-Claire Jean, Linda Karsteter, Karen Nichols, Betty Teller, Scott Willett, and Allegra Wright. SITES is also grateful to Elisabeth Brummer, Mark Gulezian, Neil Trager, and Susan Weidman.

Books have a life far beyond that of a single museum exhibition. Producing this one was unusually challenging, in part because it involved writers on both sides of the Atlantic, but also because it was based on ever-changing political conditions. SITES editor Melissa Hirsch responded to these challenges with skill and sensitivity. We hope that *Art as Activist* will provide a context for learning more about the spirited creativity that ushered in a new Europe.

Anna R. Cohn, Director
and Crisley McCarson, Project Director
Smithsonian Institution Traveling Exhibition Service

THE AGE OF THE POSTER

ISTVÁN OROSZ

*Poster designer and
animated film director
Hungary*

In June 1990, I was asked by the curators of *Art as Activist* to write an essay about the posters created during the recent revolutions in Central and Eastern Europe. I have been haunted ever since by the thought that I may be writing not a foreword, but an epilogue; that this may be the swan song of the poster.

The political upheavals that progressed country by country in this part of the world were euphoric moments in history. I would count among those moments the revitalization of the poster. For months we were red-eyed from lack of sleep, and these months revived the poster contrary to all recent trends.

One must remember that the poster had not been very important for years either as a means of conveying information or as an art form. Television, radio, and newspapers had so overwhelmed posters that the dictatorships were convinced it was enough to be concerned with mass media alone. There probably was not even a proper department in our ministries of interior to maintain files on poster designers. Perhaps they were just lumped together under "P" with "plagiarists" and "primrose cultivators." In the arts as well the poster rarely has been more than a subservient accompaniment to a play or film.

Then, for a few odd months, everything changed in the cities and towns from the Danube to the Black Sea. People shut off their television sets and ventured into the streets. They began reading broadsides pasted up on walls, then holding aloft placards. When they turned to one another, they no longer thought, as they previously did, that their compatriot was dressed as a civilian only to deceive. On posters they beheld repressed longings that they had not dared pronounce in more than forty years. The poster became—as it had been in its first heroic age— disturbing, demanding, and memorable. Film, theater, exhibitions, and even commercial posters followed suit with revolutionary changes. No more "socialist realism." No more taboo subjects. The three artistic categories of the regime—approved, tolerated, and forbidden—ceased to exist.

Krzysztof Ducki, the young Polish poster designer living in Hungary, put it this way, "The barrier now is not between permitted and forbidden thought, it is between two artists' groups. One has something to say, the other does not."

Poster artists who had been bursting with unpublishable ideas for years, perhaps decades, came forward, cautiously at first, then with increasing boldness, raising their voices against funding for an environmentally disastrous project, then for the rights of ethnic minorities. They supported the reestablishment of the old national emblems and went on to attack the Party's corruption. They demanded recognition of people's uprisings from times past and the rehabilitation of executed revolutionary leaders. As courage rose, they approached the touchiest of all subjects—the departure of Soviet forces.

Despite heavily guarded borders, posters became traveling ambassadors of the arts. Artists took their trade from city to city, making sure that posters would document critical events as they unfolded. Polish artist Ducki commented with native fluency on Hungarian events, as did Hungarian Péter Pócs about German

Untitled

*Egils Vitols
Latvia, 1989
Gouache*

Riga's monument of freedom is either rising or drowning, a comment on the uncertainty of Latvia's future.

and Romanian revolts. During the Czech revolution, Ducki, Pócs, Pinczehelyi, and I made our way to Prague and to Brno. Our freshly baked ideas were reproduced by the hands of the Czech students in the evening. By the next morning the messages of Hungarian posterists were in the streets.

It is common knowledge that revolutions are not made by professional politicians, especially not in these parts. Politicians tend to return when things are stabilized enough to tell who is winning. It is the writers, the poets, the artists who are likely to be at the forefront. It was they who sensed first in Warsaw and Prague, in Vilnius and Budapest, when the time had come.

In 1848, Europe was swept by a wave of revolutions not unlike today. "The time is now, now or never!" wrote the great poet Sándor Petőfi, lighting the flame of revolution in Hungary. Not only the poem, but the very typeface in which it was set on flyers came to pose a threat to dictatorships. Today, it is the *Solidarnosc* logotype that incites that kind of passion in Poland and beyond.

The euphoria will pass, and the significance of the art will diminish. It will no longer cause upheaval, neither will it be what it was under dictatorship, when the arts alone reminded us of freedoms past and imagined. In the bourgeois democracy to come, the arts will return to conforming with generally accepted definitions and, even more, they will become commodities. As to the rest, it will be nice to remember some day that there was a time in Central and Eastern Europe that might be termed "The Age of the Poster."

THE ART OF THE STREET

MARTA SYLVESTROVÁ
Curator
Moravian Gallery
Brno, Czechoslovakia

Life in a totalitarian society had two faces, the official and the private. The first was public, controlled and seemingly loyal to the regime; the other was critical, but confined within the family or to a small circle of independent groups. The "two-facedness" of everyday reality was reflected in the evolution of posters, as well as in art, theater, music, and literature. And yet it was only posters, "the art of the street," that became instant historical documents, recording the political and social changes of the day. I witnessed many of these historic moments personally, as I traveled across Central and Eastern Europe in 1989–90, collecting posters for this exhibition.

In liberal democracies such as America, poster art is overshadowed by television, broadcasting, film, and video. However, under the totalitarian regimes of Central and Eastern Europe, all mass communications were under strict control of the governments; the way to communicate unofficial ideas was through posters, leaflets, and banners, "samizdat" literature, and other forms of underground culture. The censoring authorities could not stop the production of hand drawn and privately printed posters appearing and reappearing on the streets, walls, and windows of the cities and towns during anti-totalitarian revolts.

Artists worked under the difficult conditions of government censorship. Artists living in such conditions of censorship and self-censorship hid their meaning behind symbols, and their criticism in metaphors. Their creations drew attention to forbidden spiritual values and criticized totalitarian states in which the absurdity of Orwell's vision and Kafka's existentialism had been realized. Official Marxist ideology embraced socialist realism as the basic art style for a socialist society. "Socrealism," a poster by Russian artist Gosha Kamenskich (page

Berlin exhibition, Nov. 4, 1989. Photo by Manfred Butzmann.

134), shows how the official artistic style fettered artistic imagination, because its proponents condemned as "formalistic" any non-figurative work.

Under such conditions, the official political poster lost its artistic value. It succumbed to the pressure of commissions and to the ideology of controlling offices; it served the ideals of the ruling Communist party. It resorted to time-worn themes and cliches, celebrating Marxist-Leninism and contemporary party leaders.

Although official political posters degenerated, political content was preserved in some cultural posters, where artful symbolism often passed by the eyes of the censors, if only for a short time. In Poland, the artist E. Get-Stankiewicz juxtaposed his own self-portrait against "red power" symbols in his theater posters. In one poster he is strangled by a big red cat. This slipped by the official censors, but a similar reference did not. It was a poster for "Dziady" or "Forefather's Eve," a play by M. A. Mickiewicz about Russian hegemony over Poland during the 19th century (page 147). Get-Stankiewicz painted himself on a red background like Lenin and again, in another drawn portrait, being crushed by a red square. The symbolism was so evident that the poster was forbidden and could not be put up in the streets. A similar fate befell the play after a protest by the Russian ambassador in Warsaw, who considered it anti-Russian provocation. After 1968, "Dziady" was banned for several years by the censors.

In order to communicate with the world beyond the strictly guarded frontiers of the totalitarian states, graphic artists participated in international poster exhibitions. The Brno and Warsaw Biennials were among the pioneers. The increasing number of international shows (Paris, Mexico City, Fort Collins, Colorado etc.) motivated the graphic artists toward independent creation, even though, in order to register, they had to survive the committee siftings of official and national guilds. The yearning for personal expression and the desire to react truthfully to the problems of society led graphic artists to create so-called "author's posters." These were published in limited editions of 10 to 250 pieces, lithographed or silk-screened at the artist's own expense. Such designs did not have to be approved by any committees, and the reproduction was ordered only through the artists who were directly in touch with the printing office. There were some ideas which no printer had the courage to produce, and so only the originals remain.

An example of such a work is Jan Sawka's "Car of the Year" (page 43), an original gouache painting in three panels, which won first prize at the 1978 Warsaw International Poster Biennial. Ten years after the invasion of Czechoslovakia by five "brotherly" armies, Sawka expressed this personal protest against using tanks to intimidate rebelling citizens.

Original "artist's posters" created during the period of *perestroika* and *glasnost* in the Soviet Union constitute a very specific phenomenon. I discovered them during my first visit to the Baltic Coast in August 1988, where I had traveled to participate in the Poster Fest at Cesis, near Riga, Latvia. Printed posters were installed on panels in the streets of the town. "As You Work, So Shall You Be Rewarded" (page 63), an ironic poster by Yurís Dimiters, dominated the space just beneath a big statue of V. I. Lenin. Most of the posters were either political or

ecological in nature and openly criticized the defects of the Communist system. This was the real *glasnost,* and yet one could still be punished for it in my native Czechoslovakia.

Increasing national pride was evident at the festival in Cesis. Latvian national symbols, forbidden for decades, appeared in the streets as well as on original posters. Two days later, in Riga, one of the first permitted demonstrations occurred around the Latvian Statue of Liberty, with demonstrators carrying posters calling for independence. Friends told me, "It was created from donations by the Latvian people in 1938, and for us became a symbol of Latvian independence." For many years, citizens put flowers and candles at the base of the statue to commemorate the victims of Stalinism. Police always arrested people who lingered too long. Now the statue was crowded with demonstrators carrying crude reproductions of a poster by Gunárs Lusis that depicted Stalin and Hitler cutting up Europe, with a red star overlaying a fascist cross. It was titled, "Friendship '39."

I decided to collect these Latvian posters, in the hope that I could exhibit them in Czechoslovakia, where fear of consequences still silenced many artists. After my stay in Riga, I continued on to Tallinn, the capital of Estonia, and then to Leningrad, where a new spirit existed among a group of young designers born in the 1950s. In 1988, Leningrad poster artists held two exhibitions of original posters that the Communist authorities tried to close. Masses of visitors, however,

Curator Marta Sylvestrová and artist Gunárs Lusis marched in this demonstration for Latvian independence. Riga, Jan. 25, 1991. Photo by Uldis Briedis.

Romanian demonstrators after seizing a tank, Bucharest, Dec. 12, 1989. Photo by Jan Šibík.

stood in front of the exhibition hall awaiting the opening, which caused the authorities to not only open the exhibit, but extend its run.

In support of Gorbachev's *perestroika* and *glasnost,* Russian graphic artists originated visual images, which were more effective psychologically than reading words in newspaper articles or listening to radio and TV speeches about the same. Simple humorous ideas were expressed in photomontages by masterful artists such as Alexander Faldin and Rashit Akmanov (page 70), who ridiculed previously inviolable politicians and party leaders.

I carried mostly photomontage posters from Leningrad back to Brno and soon opened the first *perestroika* poster exhibition at the Moravian Gallery in November 1988. The title, "*Perestroika,*" was not permitted and I was not allowed to reproduce for the exhibition invitation Faldin's poster, "Bravo!" (page 78), an image of Gorbachev literally conducting a news program. I was not allowed to exhibit some of the rare posters I had collected. How dangerous art can be!

"Who, if not us? When, if not now?" With this slogan, people in Poland, Hungary, East Germany, Bulgaria, Czechoslovakia, and Romania took part in mass demonstrations during the watershed year of 1989. Communist rule and the centralized system of economy had brought the countries of the Eastern Bloc to the brink of economic, social, and political crisis. Gorbachev's reform program had tried to change the Communist dictatorship into a human political system with a functioning economy, yet the failure of reformist measures during the Hungarian Fall of 1956, Prague Spring in 1968, and the Polish Solidarity Movement in 1980–81, which had all been crushed by military power, shook the trust of the people in Communist reforms.

As the people's revolutions swept across Central Europe, the long period of "two-facedness" ended, and an open political fight began. The poster played an unforgettable role in this struggle. Not only professional artists, but anonymous amateurs used posters to express their opinions and to attack the totalitarian regime in the hope of its defeat. With humorous slogans, broad symbols, and striking pictures, the posters invited passersby to stop, look, and participate. The efforts of the people's militia, state police, and their confidants to tear down the posters were futile. As soon as the posters were torn down, they would reappear overnight or within hours. The images were already fixed in the minds of the people and drawn again by anonymous hands.

Posters were everywhere—on shop windows, taped on walls, dangling from city monuments. People pinned them on their own bodies and carried them in demonstrations. During the "Velvet Revolution," Prague students covered a train with posters, bringing news to remote villages and towns concerning the brutal police action against the student demonstrators, the strike, and the founding of Civic Forum. The train posters served as an invitation to the local residents to join in the strike.

"No Democratization, but Democracy!" The cries of demonstrators were mirrored on city walls, helping to sustain revolutionary enthusiasm. Forbidden national symbols appeared; new symbols of the revolutionary movements and opposition parties helped to unify their struggles. The smiling "happy face" in an "OF" represented the Czech Civic Forum; it was designed by Pavel Šťastný, one

Many East Germans such as Gübig did not wish to be consumed by the capitalist West.

of the striking students at the Academy of Applied Arts in Prague, as a symbol of a happier future. The emblem of three flying birds in the Hungarian national colors was created by Gyorgy Kara for the SZDSZ, or Alliance of Free Democrats. The *Solidarnosc* logotype, first drawn in 1980 by Jerzy Janiszewski in Gdansk, served as a unifying symbol not only in the Polish revolution, but in the elections that put Wałesa in office.

While television and other mass media were still fighting against old political authorities for a new face, the poster provided a spontaneous and vivid account of daily events. Its language was direct, and its images were persuasive and crude, caricaturing old party leaders. On revolutionary banners, East German leader Erich Honecker's official state portrait looked out from behind jail bars. Romanian dictator Nicola Ceauşescu was drawn with a bloody vampire grimace. The image of Miloš Jakeš, the titular head of state in Czechoslovakia, appeared with his typical smirk and was crowned with a fool's bell cap.

Later, when the Communist party replaced old leaders with new "puppet leaders," the posters spoke out against them. The poster became the mediator of popular emotions, stimulating the growing clamor for radical reforms, proclaiming the passion of spontaneous meetings and mass demonstrations. The major event of 1989 occurred on November 9th, when crowds began to tear down the Berlin Wall. The hated symbol of an ideologically divided world fell, opening the way for a speedy reunification of Germany. The blank Wall had always tempted poster artists. On the surface of the west side, artists drew images of the long-standing desire for freedom; on the east side, any such attempts were considered political provocation and were painted over immediately. Often the mounting of posters resulted in punitive action. "Once I photographed all the dead trees in East Berlin and composed them on a

Untitled

Anonymous
Romania, 1989
Original Drawing

Each day, passers-by added
graffiti to this poster of
Ceauşescu, Romanian
dictator.

poster," said artist Manfred Butzmann, whose underground activities included environmental concerns. "For that my works were banned for two years." The exuberant posters from the period during the removal of the Wall also convey a nervousness about its outcome; East German posters refer to the problem of being swallowed up by their strong and wealthy neighbor, West Germany, during the reunification process.

As the revolutionary movements traveled from one country to the next, sweeping out the Communist regimes, the poster became a kind of traveling ambassador, supporting them all. Poster artists traveled around to support the various revolutions. For example, DOPP, a group of Hungarian poster artists, created campaign posters for the Hungarian Democratic Forum, an opposi-

The fall of the Wall,
Germany, Nov. 11, 1989.
Photo by Jan Šibík.

tion party in their own country, and then traveled to Brno and Prague to produce posters for the "Velvet Revolution." I invited DOPP to exhibit their work in Brno, but when artist István Orosz saw their posters the next day plastered on the walls and windows of the city, he said, "*This* is the best place for our exhibition!"

After this comment, I began to think about an exhibition that would serve as a spontaneous record of the exciting days in Central and Eastern Europe. In the spring of 1990, Dana Bartelt, curator of the traveling exhibition, *Contemporary Czechoslovak Posters*, invited me to lecture in the United States, and we decided to collaborate on *Art as Activist*. However, to complete the collection from the Moravian Gallery, I knew that I would need to travel into the Soviet Union, through the Ukraine to Lithuania and Latvia, where original, unpublished posters were still in the hands of poster artists.

I arrived in Vilnius in January 1991, only a few days after the night assault by OMON, the special Soviet black beret forces, on the TV tower and broadcasting station. Mass demonstrations were being held at the TV tower and nearby at the Lithuanian Parliament. "A small TV tower in Kaunas called for help for Vilnius," I was told by graphic artist Juazos Galkus. "People from all over Lithuania came the day after the attack to protect the Parliament building; about 80,000 citizens made a human chain with linked hands, making a decision for freedom or death." Fires were still burning when I arrived at the site. There were still iron barriers around the Parliament, covered with hand-painted posters, especially children's drawings and watercolors. One of the children's drawings showed soldiers shooting people in the back; two others portrayed a lady in black standing near a grave with candles, and a girl hoisting a flag on top of Gedeminas castle, a symbol of the previous, independent monarchy. "Lithuania will be free!" was written on many amateur posters.

In Riga, a similar atmosphere existed. Gunárs Lusis, a graphic artist who helped gather many of the original Latvian posters in the exhibition, was in mourning for his friend Andris Slapins, a poet and film director, who had been shot during an OMON night attack while he was filming a documentary. "It's heartbreaking," Lusis said. "We were together at Christmas. It doesn't make sense why he and others had to die." Slapins's last, unfinished poem read:

It's a dark night
He stands on guard
and the ground moves like in a fight
Starry cape veils the night ceiling
with morning stars
and you look across the edge of your pit
how your neighbor digs himself a grave

Most of the posters Lusis collected were painted originals. Many testified to the mass deportations and executions that took place during the Stalinist years of terror in the Baltic States. "Nearly everyone lost a family member during that time," Lusis told me. "Several nationalities were erased from the map of the Soviet Union by the Bolshevik power. Our historical monuments were ruined; churches changed into storehouses; cafes into public toilets, or, in more favorable decisions, into galleries. The National House of Culture was confiscated for the Soviet Army." In the Latvian posters of 1989, national symbols, so long suppressed, appear in richly hand-painted posters. Egils Vítols's poster shows the Latvian Statue of Liberty (page 10) either sinking or emerging, an image that signifies the uncertainty of the nation's future. In another poster by Vilnis Piķis, the red wall of the Kremlin, a symbol of Soviet hegemony over the Baltic States, is broken through by the morning star, the national symbol of Latvia (page 2).

Latvian and Lithuanian posters inspired Polish graphic designers, who were heirs to a long tradition of painted posters. The "School of the Polish Art Poster" gained international renown in the 1970s for its irony and influenced cultural posters throughout Central and Eastern Europe. Many Polish poster artists, as in other parts of the Eastern Bloc, were trained as painters, architects, and set designers. Drawing from their knowledge of the modern styles of surrealism, pop and op-art, neo-Art Nouveau, new expressionism, and others, they composed posters with dazzling visual metaphors.

Most of the Polish poster artists sympathized with Solidarity, the trade union movement. Jan Sawka, living in exile in the United States, created "Solidarity," a poster that helped raise money for Polish underground activity (page 48). Piotr Młodożeniec reprinted by hand his leaflets and posters in support of Solidarity to help political prisoners after the declaration of martial law. During the presidential campaign, Młodożeniec used Wałęsa's initials "LW" to create a caricature of him (page 121).

At the last moment, right before we finalized the collection for *Art as Activist*, I was visited in Brno by Andrei Kolosov and Valeria Kovrigina, who hand delivered original posters from Moscow. "There is no publisher who will print our political posters," Kolosov said. "Previously, the Poster Publishing House of the Central Committee of the Communist Party produced state propaganda posters; now to be more profitable, they have turned to the production of very commercial sex magazines. So now I print my posters and those of my friends by silkscreen in my studio."

The posters he delivered have great strength in their pungent satire and dramatic images. Lenin is given the Devil's look (page 132). "In the beginning of *perestroika*," graphic artist Dimitri Surski explains, "it seemed that we were returning to Lenin's ideology. But when the archives were opened and the truth of Lenin's life was published, we learned that it was his decision to execute the family of the Czar as well as many religious dignitaries and priests. We understood that the evil really began with Lenin." These Russian posters convey uncertainty, not just about the past, but the future.

The tense atmosphere and revolutionary euphoria disappeared soon after victory was achieved. The opposition won against the Communists in free elections in Poland, Czechoslovakia, Hungary, East Germany, Slovenia, and Croatia during the years 1989–90. In Bulgaria, the Communists stayed in power even after the elections, and it took another six months of student and worker's strikes to form a coalition government. The complicated situation in Romania has yet to be resolved. In the presidential elections that followed sweeping political

**Democracy! Pluralism!
Glasnost!**
Alexander Chantsev
Russia, 1990

The title refers ironically to
opposition calls for democratic pluralism in Russia.

reforms, the leading personalities of dissent were elected—Václav Havel, the first speaker and co-founder of Charter 77, in Czechoslovakia; Solidarity leader Lech Wałesa in Poland; writer and dramatist Arpad Goncz in Hungary; and writer Zelyu Zelev in Bulgaria.

People are slowly forgetting the freedomless times under former Communist regimes. Poster art has gained an altogether new condition for its development. The possibility of establishing private firms in a market economy gives graphic artists a new field in which to work; newly formed companies are looking for advertising. And yet, all this raises the question: Why did posters, during a brief period from 1989 to 1990, become a medium capable of rousing the people? Krzysztof Ducki, a Polish poster artist, explains:

> We wanted our posters to communicate and be understandable. Modern posters join idea, form, drawing, and color, and are artistic. They must follow what is happening in art and be a mediator between the street and the gallery.
>
> In the beginning of glasnost, my Russian friends still had deep fear under the skin. For politics people murder, starve. That is why political posters impress. The more truth in them, the more effective they are because they evoke deep emotions in spectators. People wept in front of posters for victims of Stalin. Such a strong reaction is never experienced with a cultural poster that invites the viewer to the theater or to films. In political posters, whoever sees must understand which side I stand on, against whom, what I want, and whom I oppose.

This openness had been impossible in previous totalitarian regimes. The "two-facedness" of posters had ended. When people realized it was possible to express themselves freely, they began to look at things differently, as if they were cleansed from the inside. Let *Art as Activist* be not only a celebration of this victory, but also a remembrance, and a resolution for a brighter future.

In November 1989, when thousands of printed and hand drawn posters expressing the real will of citizens were hanging on the walls of our towns, we recognized what power is hidden in their art.

VÁCLAV HAVEL

FOR PETER WEISS

Some time, later,
we shall break the archive seals.
Sitting together then
we shall utter what has never been said before.

On the table lay hands
no longer balled into fists.
No movement of fingers.
No one to fall on any one.

Betrayed sacrifices traitors
    trials hearings depositions charges

Some time, hopefully soon, but later,
we shall bear the whole truth.

We shall name heroic heroes
    wrong the wrong

one after another we shall announce ourselves in words
break the silence.

STEFFEN MENSCHING
East Germany

*Unless otherwise noted, all
posters are from the collection
of the Moravian Gallery,
Brno, Czechoslovakia.
All posters are printed offset
unless indicated.*

right:

1937
*Yuris Dimiters
Latvia, 1988*

1937 was a year of Stalinist
terror. Many were abducted
and shot in the back of the
head; no explanations, no
trials.

Художник Юрий Дмитриев

Фото плаката 1988. На славянском и русском языках

МПм «АГИТ» 1988

DEGREES OF BARBARIANISM

Degrees of barbarianism. This is how: first you destroy those who create values. Then you destroy those who know what values are, and who also know that those destroyed before were in fact the creators of values. But real barbarism begins when no one can any longer judge or know that what he does is barbaric.

RYSZARD KAPUŚCIŃSKI
A Warsaw Diary, 1983

Party-Comrades
Alexander Vaganov
Russia, 1990
Mixed media
Lent by Plackart

Vaganov depicts Hitler and Stalin as brothers in totalitarian politics and dictatorship. Their 1939 pact, dividing Europe into spheres of influence, permitted the Soviets to seize eastern Poland in 1939 and the Baltic republics and Bessarabia in 1940.

STALIN
(SATURN-SATAN)

He said:
Believe in me! I am time!

And when they believed in him
he devoured his children.

VLADIMIR LEVCHEV
Bulgaria

Happy Children, 1939
Andrei Kolosov & Valeria Kovrigina
Russia, 1990
Silkscreen

A gleeful Stalin and Hitler sign their historic 1939 pact.

хотелось бы ВСЕХ поименно назвать...

right:

**I Would Like to Know
All of Their Names**
Viktor Kundyshev
Russia, 1987
Photograph

Kundyshev dedicated this
poster to the millions Stalin
had executed or deported to
remote labor camps.

1941, 1949
Laimonis Shénbergs
Latvia, 1989

In 1941, called "The
Dreadful Year" in Latvia,
Stalin deported 34,000
citizens to Siberian labor
camps; a similar mass
deportation followed in
1949. The three stars
represent Latvia's three
major regions.

THEY WILL HAVE EYES TO SEE

they will have eyes to see and they will not see
neither ridges of mist nor fruitstone nor root
neither darkness of raven nor bleaching bones
will they see

they will have ears to hear and they will not hear
neither grass sprouting during the endless nights
nor the prophetic song of the honey-tongued nightingale
will they hear

they will have tongues to speak and they will not utter
a single word to river tree mist or stone
not a brass farthing in the mane of hell
will they utter

but the wound of this field will not close
sown with dragon's teeth

JURIS KUNNOSS
Latvia

Untitled
Pyotr Kapustin
Russia, 1988
Photographic print

Soviet leader Nikita
Khrushchev's mechanized
state farms threatened the
traditional farming style of
rural Russia.

THEOLOGY OF HOPELESSNESS

God is something very
small
and transient.

It trembles inside us.

Outside is death.

But if a man
sings out
when stood against the wall—
isn't he greater than death?

For isn't man
stood against the wall?

Let him sing!

VLADIMIR LEVCHEV
Bulgaria

Untitled
Ziegfried Rischar
East Germany, 1989

This photograph won a prize
in the *Overcoming the Wall
by Painting the Wall*
exhibition organized by the
museum at Checkpoint
Charlie in West Berlin.

11. KONGRES SKH

**11th Congress of the
Croatian Union of the
Communist Party**
*Boris Ljubicic
Yugoslavia, 1989*

The 11th Congress was the
last held by the Communist
Party before it was dissolved
in Croatia. The artist depicts
rigid Bolshevik thinking in a
forehead made of stone.

right:

Imre Nagy
*Krzysztof Ducki
Hungary, 1989
Silkscreen*

A memorial to the executed
leader of the 1956 Hungarian revolution.

QUESTION AND ANSWER

In *The Resurrection,* Tolstoy writes: "Suppose we had to solve the following psychological problem: How to make the people of our time, Christians, humanitarians—in other words, good people—perpetrate the most awful villainies without feeling a sense of guilt?" There is only one possibility: make them satraps, prison governors, officers, and policemen. That is, they would have to be convinced, first, that there is an institution called government service that treats people as objects, as deserving no humane brotherly treatment, and second, that government service should be organized so that the responsibility for the outcome of treating people in this way will not fall on any one individual. These are the only conditions under which it is possible in our time to perpetrate the cruelties I have witnessed today.

RYSZARD KAPUŚCIŃSKI
A Warsaw Diary, 1983

301-SZDSZ
Péter Pócs & László Haris
Hungary, 1989

The bloody map of Hungary with a symbolic crucifix evokes the repression following the failed 1956 revolution. The number "301" marks the mass grave entombing revolutionary leader Imre Nagy. "SZDSZ" are the initials of a new Hungarian political party— the Alliance of Free Democrats.

Oct. 23, 1956
Péter Pócs
Hungary, 1989

Pócs's mouse trap recalls the first day of the 1956 Hungarian revolution, ultimately crushed by Soviet troops.

HOW TO STAGE A MODERN COUP

A scenario: a *coup d'état*. It takes place at dawn; the city is sleeping. A tank and only one tank—the country is small, the army limited and badly equipped—and two lorries of soldiers stop outside the television station. A drowsy sentry in his box by the gate. It is dark and the main building is empty. Gradually the technicians, engineers, camera and lighting men arrive. They are bewildered and frightened. The building comes alive. There is activity in the corridors and the studio. At dawn the announcer reads the first communiques and directives of the new rulers.

The palace during the same hours. No one now takes any notice of the president. Messengers cross the city informing ministers that the president awaits them—some arrive, some don't. In the palace the atmosphere is one of nervousness, fear, imminent apocalypse. All appeal is rushed to the nation, reminding it of the sole legal authority. But the appeal remains a scrap of paper, unknown to anyone outside the palace; the television and radio as well as the editorial offices of the country's sole newspaper are now in the hands of the conspirators. The president and his entourage, placed outside the sphere of action, have ceased to exist. The conspirators have established their headquarters in the television building from which they now issue their decrees and commands. The importance of the *coup d'état*: the object attacked is not the palace but the television building.

RYSZARD KAPUŚCIŃSKI
A Warsaw Diary, 1983

Car of the Year
Jan Sawka
Poland, 1978
Gouache

This poster won first prize in
the Warsaw Biennial.

UNDER THE CANNONS

Prague students made posters wherever possible—on the ground, on the pavements, on the grass, all over. Fiery slogans and appeals of resistance were very often drawn right under the cannons of the tanks.

At that time we did not know that the names of the hated collaborator—a list hung on every street corner under the old regime—would become the names of our leading statesmen.

JINDRICH MARCO
Artist, Czechoslovakia

Prague 68
Krzysztof Ducki
Hungary, 1989
Silkscreen

Ducki was in Prague when the Czech revolution broke out in November 1989. This poster recalls the Prague Spring, Czechoslovakia's brief period of liberalization in 1968, cut short by invading tanks from the Warsaw Pact countries.

IS THERE A FUTURE FOR THE CZECH POLITICAL POSTER?

In the 1950s, Czech cities were overflowing with "political" posters. They proclaimed May Day, Children's Day, Women's Day, Day of the Railroad Workers, or just reassured us that our tomorrow with the Soviet Union is bright and beautiful. After a short while, nobody paid any attention to these posters; and to Western visitors they signified the atmosphere of the eastern part of Europe, they told them how we decorate our cities (quite expensively, by the way).

In the 1960s, however, we began to feel the time had passed for just wasting printed paper; if a "political poster" must exist, then let it speak to somebody, let it make people think. In this spirit, five artists founded the Plakart poster group in 1962. They set out to stage a renaissance of the real political poster, a poster in the spirit of humanism. Although Western Europeans admired these creations, they never reached the streets of Czechoslovak cities.

Then the spring and August of 1968 came. The first days of the occupation and general resistance toward the invaders were also the days of the political poster. The more these were created anonymously and without much regard to art, the more they were convincing on the fences, walls, and pieces of wrapping paper where everyone saw them. At the print shops, nobody needed an order or the approval stamps. They took the designs out of my hands and worked on them nonstop and overnight. The next day, while Russian tanks were standing in front of the shop and Russian troops were occupying one of the print shops, the posters were whisked out of a back entrance disguised as a garbage collection point.

Two decades later, the November 17, 1989, massacre on Národni Třída in Prague again produced an immediate reaction. Prague was flooded with witty homemade leaflets and signs. Before creating new posters, I dusted off some of my 1968 "Eye With a Bloody Tear" posters, wrote in a new date by hand, and took them where the opposition was being born, to Prague theaters and universities.

As for the future of the political poster: in a developed totalitarian society, a sensible, critical political poster is unacceptable to the state because it is destabiliz- ing. In a developed democratic society, even if it does not threaten the establishment, the poster will not find a publisher, except in the political opposition. Today, politicians use television and radio to influence citizens. In these mass media every problem can be discussed in its own complexity, which the political poster cannot do. Because Czechoslovakia wants to enter the family of prosperous European cities, I think that the real political poster already bid goodbye to Czechoslovakia.

VÁCLAV ŠEVČÍK
Artist, Czechoslovakia

Aug. 21, 1968
Nov. 17, 1989
Václav Ševčík
Czechoslovakia, 1968, 1989
(Nov. 17, 1989 *lent by*
Dana Bartelt)

In his 1968 poster, Ševčík condemned the invasion of troops to suppress the Prague Spring. Twenty-one years later, he added a reference to the Czech revolution of 1989.

Solidarity
Jan Sawka
U.S.A., 1982

Exiled Polish artist Jan
Sawka produced this
fundraising poster for the
Solidarity movement.

Emigrants

Stasys Eidrigevičius
Poland, 1990

In this theater poster, the use of *wrona*—Polish for "ravens" (or "big, black ugly birds")—alludes to the acronym for the Polish Military Council for National Salvation (WRON). When martial law was declared in 1981, this council eliminated the jobs of Solidarity workers. In 1990, after the Solidarity victory, the supporters of WRON are depicted leaving their jobs.

HOMO SOVETICUS

right:

Homo Soveticus
Dimitri Surski & Tatyana
Gardashnikova
Russia, 1989

The artists refer to Stalin's
quote, "All people are just a
single screw in the great
machine."

**The Deportee's
Creation**
Gintaras Gesevichius
Lithuania, 1989

The Hill of Crosses, near
Siauliai, has symbolized
resistance for Lithuanians
since the 19th century. After
Communist leaders razed
the site in 1961 and 1975,
the crosses reappeared
overnight.

REPORT FROM A BESIEGED CITY

Too old to carry arms and to fight like others—

they generously assigned to me the inferior role of a chronicler
I record—not knowing for whom—the history of the siege

I have to be precise but I don't know when the invasion began
two hundred years ago in December in autumn perhaps yesterday at dawn
here everybody is losing the sense of time

we were left with the place an attachment to the place
still we keep ruins of temples phantoms of gardens of houses
if we were to lose the ruins we would be left with nothing

I write as I can in the rhythm of unending weeks
monday: storehouses are empty a rat is now a unit of currency
tuesday: the mayor is killed by unknown assailants
wednesday: talks of armistice the enemy interned our envoys
we don't know where they are being kept i.e. tortured
thursday: after a stormy meeting the majority voted down
the motion of spice merchants on unconditional surrender
friday: the onset of plague
saturday: the suicide of
N. N., the most steadfast defender

sunday: no water we repulsed
the attack at the eastern gate named the Gate of Alliance

I know all this is monotonous nobody would care

I avoid comments keep emotions under control describe facts
they say facts only are valued on foreign markets
but with a certain pride I wish to convey to the world
thanks to the war we raised a new species of children
our children don't like fairy tales they play killing
day and night they dream of soup bread bones
exactly like dogs and cats

(continues on p. 54)

Untitled
J. W. Huber
East Germany, 1989

Onto a modern apartment Huber superimposes a 19th-century painting of a man with flowers, a reminder of the warmer, more personal life of the past.

in the evening I like to wander in the confines of the City
along the frontiers of our uncertain freedom
I look from above on the multitude of armies on their lights
I listen to the din of drums to barbaric shrieks
it's incredible that the City is still resisting
the siege has been long the foes must replace each other
they have nothing in common except a desire to destroy us
the Goths the Tartars the Swedes the Emperor's troops regiments of
    Our Lord's Transfiguration
who could count them
colors of banners change as does the forest on the horizon
from the bird's delicate yellow in the spring through the green the red
    to the winter black
and so in the evening freed from facts I am able to give thought
to bygone far away matters for instance to our
allies overseas I know they feel true compassion
they send us flour sacks of comfort lard and good counsel
without even realizing that we were betrayed by their fathers
our former allies from the time of the second Apocalypse
their sons are not guilty they deserve our gratitude so we are grateful
they have never lived through the eternity of a siege
those marked by misfortune are always alone
Dalai Lama's defenders Kurds Afghan mountaineers

now as I write these words proponents of compromise
have won a slight advantage over the party of the dauntless
unusual shifts of mood our fate is still in the balance

cemeteries grow larger the number of defenders shrinks
but the defense continues and will last to the end
and even if the City falls and one of us survives
he will carry the City inside him on the roads of exile
he will be the City

we look at the face of hunger the face of fire the face of death
and the worst of them all—the face of treason

and only our dreams have not been humiliated

ZBIGNIEW HERBERT
Poland, 1982
Translated by Czesław Miłosz

SCÉNÁŘ / IVO KROBOT A PETR OSLZLÝ   REŽIE / IVO KROBOT   DRAMATURGIE / PETR OSLZLÝ   HUDBA / JIŘÍ BULIS

BOHUMIL HRABAL
STÁTNÍ DIVADLO BRNO
DIVADLO NA PROVÁZKU

rozvzpomínání

Memories
Joska Skálník
Czechoslovakia, 1987
Lent by Dana Bartelt

The Czech regime banned Bohumil Hrabel's book, *I Served the English King,* about the fate of the country's millionaires after the Communist takeover in 1948. This poster announces a play based on it to be performed by the avant garde Theater-on-a-String in Brno. Skálník and several members of the company were imprisoned for their participation. He later became an advisor to President Havel.

Golden Era/Chocolate, Vodka, Coca-Cola, Bananas, Oranges/ Black Bread

Maria Rus
Romania, 1990
Mixed media

In the first panel, Rus uses black bread and an onion as a metaphor for the misery of everyday life in Ceaușescu's "Golden Era." The second panel depicts food items that were unattainable luxuries in the 1980s. Finally, she shows only black bread—foreshadowing Romania's dark future.

Ceva....
Ciocolată
Vodcă
Coca-Cola
Banane
Portocale
Lămâie
Cafeaua
Ce-ai...

HAT

This elderly gentleman
also takes walks in the Yard
But his hat clashes
with the barbed wire
and the bars muzzling the windows
as though they were afraid we might bite through
This man with a hat
is here because he sought
to overthrow the government by force
and violate our treaties

Sixty years old
his hands furrowed like the earth
of pre-war Europe
and a very dangerous hat
on his head.

TOMASZ JASTRUN
Poland

The Dream Brigade
Krzysztof Ducki
Hungary, 1988

In this poster for a film condemning the Communist work camps of the 1950s, Ducki transforms the Crown of St. Stephen (a symbol of the Hungarian kingdom) into a prison beret.

vienbalsīgi... единогласно...

right:

Unanimously

Pēteris Chivlis
Latvia, 1988
Silkscreen

The decision-making process
of totalitarianism is satirized.

Vernissage

Karel Haloun
Czechoslovakia, 1990
Silkscreen

A poster for a play by Václav
Havel. Before the revolution,
all of Havel's plays were
banned in Czechoslovakia.

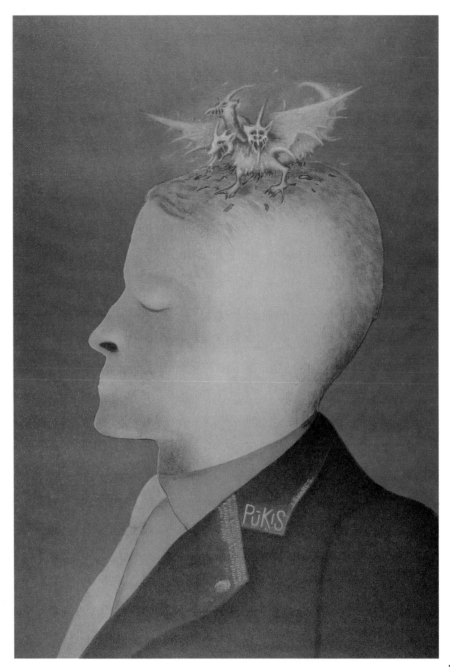

The Dragon
Ilmárs Blumbergs
Latvia, 1985

In this theater poster, Blumbergs camouflaged his political beliefs in metaphor to avoid censorship—a red dragon to convey Communist ideology.

right:

As You Work, So Shall You Be Rewarded
Yurís Dimiters
Latvia, 1987

The artist suggests that the Soviet system awards meaningless medals for worthless work.

KĀDS DARBS — TĀDA ALGA

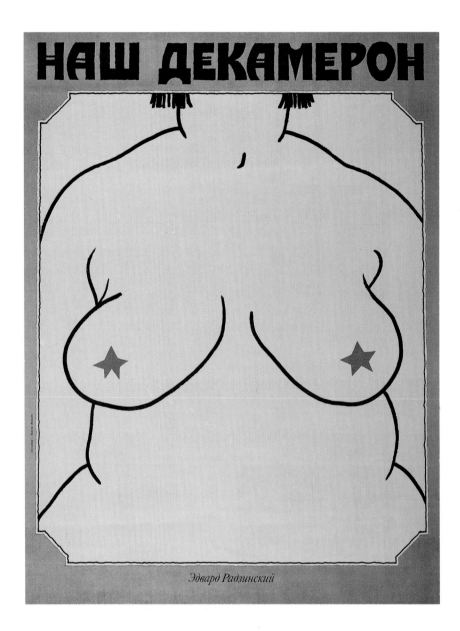

НАШ ДЕКАМЕРОН

Эдвард Радзинский

Our _Decameron_
Viktor Yakovlev
Russia, 1989

Yakovlev's Soviet woman
arose from imagery in the
Decameron, Boccaccio's
collection of bawdy tales
from the 14th century.

right:

**To Forget History Risks
Repeating It**
Alexander Faldin
Russia, 1987
Photographic print

The cult of personality
surrounding Soviet leader
Leonid Brezhnev exagger-
ated his military exploits in
WWII. The artist's halo over
an empty uniform suggests
that idolization is part of a
totalitarian system.

ЗАБВЕНИЕ ПРОШЛОГО ГРОЗИТ ЕГО ПОВТОРЕНИЕМ!

LANGUAGE BATTLES

The struggle for the future of the world—and our consciousness in it—will take place more and more in the realm of language. Language battles, battles with words, are a part of the whole of human history, but, with the advent of the mass media, they have become more intense.

RYSZARD KAPUŚCIŃSKI
A Warsaw Diary, 1983

**§O§/Criticism/
Reckoning**
*Zlatan Dryanov
Bulgaria, 1987*

Dryanov makes a visual pun: "§" is the Bulgarian symbol for a written law; "§O§" resembles the international distress symbol "SOS," thereby alluding to legal injustices. In the second panel, "Criticism," he shows that in a totalitarian regime criticism can be turned against the critic. The last panel, "Reckoning," suggests that criticism ultimately will lead to a reckoning.

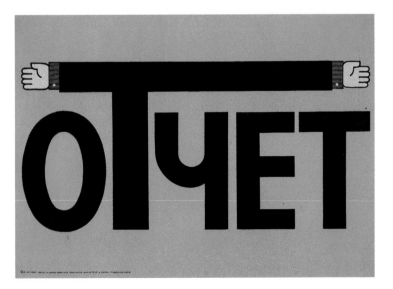

TO BEAR THE TRUTH

Some believe that by withdrawing from areas of public activity—by simply diminishing their presence—they will increase the extent of the liberty they can privately enjoy. So they strive to shrink, to impoverish themselves, and turn into dust. They expect the authorities to lose interest; for them, only those who are visible exist or those with something that can be taken away.

We follow mystics. They know where they are going. They, too, go astray, but when they go astray they do so in a way that is mystical, dark, and mysterious. This attracts us.

RYSZARD KAPUŚCIŃSKI
A Warsaw Diary, 1983

The State Needs Hard Currency
Rashit Akmanov
Russia, 1989
Mixed media

The hardships of Soviet life are exposed.

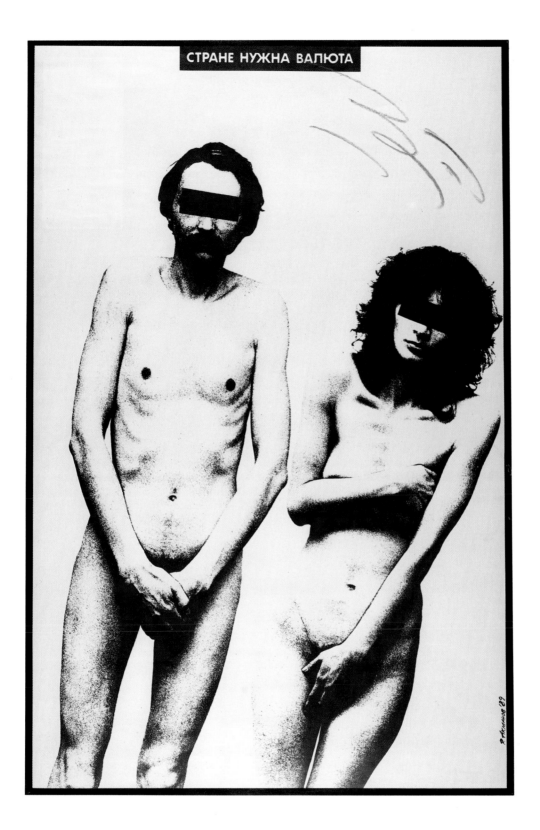

Happy Birthday, Komsomol!

Alexander Faldin & Rashit Akmanov
Russia, 1988
Mixed media

The artists find irony in Communist youth groups—in the "old-thinking" leaders behind them. The red scarf symbolizes the red kerchief worn by the Young Pioneers.

Afghanistan
*Vladimir Chesler & Sergei
Voychenko
Byelorussia, 1989*

The artists protest Soviet
aggression in Afghanistan by
commemorating the soldiers
who died there.

ШУТКА...

right:

The Joke
Vitali Levchenko
Russia, 1987
Gouache

Young West German Mathias Rust landed a small plane in Moscow's Red Square, having flown 800 miles undetected across Soviet airspace, as a "joke" on the military. Several high-ranking Soviet officers lost their jobs after the incident.

Our Children Deserve Better
J. W. Huber
East Germany, 1989

A barren children's playground in East Berlin.

from

POEMS ON MAPS

maps and calendars and maps.
time and space. time
of diaspora and dissolution
in the short dictionary of rhyme
in the blockades of besieged speech

let's leave a few names behind
the broken line of a frontier.
uncontoured, unconcerned by features
light streams from the plan, from the page
turning over us

VIKTOR KRIVULIN
Russia

Latvia
Vladimirs Naumovs
Latvia, 1990

A "map" in the form of a
wrung handkerchief
represents both Soviet
exploitation in Latvia and
the anguish of its citizens.

ONE HUNDRED METERS OF DEMOCRACY

I hadn't been in a demonstration for five years. It's nice to see friends and people one knows at these celebrations, but they, alas, had also stopped going. No one wants to waste a morning getting round pickets and barriers, finishing up in a helter of demonstrators unknown to you.

To escape all this, we decided to go to the First of May celebrations with a group of friends. Not being out to shock anyone, we chose slogans near to our hearts: "Close the Sloksky TSBK," "Let the House at No. 76 Gorky Street be for the needy," "Enough of these nests for Gentry-folk." With poster paint, white material, and a framework of bamboo poles, we were ready in a couple of evenings.

On the morning of May 1st, we joined the throng of people at the tail end of a small group enterprise. Our slogans went down well with the collective, and they took us into their ranks and offered to help carry our materials. About forty meters from the platform, a short, thickset man with an armband confronted us. This fellow, the party organizer of the group enterprise, advised us to cease our independent agitation and ran off for help. Just as "Long live *perestroika,* democracy and *glasnost!*" roared from the stage, a squad of militiamen took us out of the columns of demonstrators. Shouts of "That's democracy in action!" and "That's *glasnost* for you" rose from the ranks behind us.

We ended up in the militia station of the Kirov region. No one at the station could work out why and for what we had been brought in. We were promised that our slogans would be put before the local authorities. If, by some miracle, the local functionaries were to examine them, we would apologize for their rough-and-ready look and promise to do better next time.

As we walked back along Lenin Street, it all seemed to be OK, but an impression was left of a trick, a game, as a result of which everyone had been warned and no one would be told off. And what about the demonstrators of the group enterprise? A group of political speculators, gathering authority for themselves. No more. Let them demonstrate for themselves.

One hundred meters was about as far as we managed to get in the First of May demonstration. The militiamen themselves evaluated what our *glasnost* and cooperative festival *perestroika* was worth. But the movement is begun. If the authorities are going to remain on the platform, it will be hopelessly retarded. The marathon is ahead. We have only just begun this road, and we have to go down it to the end.

**SERGEI AND INNA PICHUGINY,
SERGEI OSKOLKOV, AND VLADIMIR IVANOV**
Latvia, September 1988

Perestroika
Assen Stareyshinski
Bulgaria, 1988

The artist shows how some
Bulgarian leaders insisted on
facing backwards even as
perestroika developed.

Bravo!
Svyetlana Faldina &
Alexander Faldin
Russia, 1988
Photograph

In this depiction of
perestroika, Soviet leader
Mikhail Gorbachev
conducts from a book of
Lenin.

Strike While the Iron Is Gorbachev

Sławomir Janiak & Witold Michorzewski
Poland, 1989

The artists play on the words "*hot*" and "*Gorbachev*"—in Polish *gorąco* and *Gorbaczow*—suggesting that the time for change is now.

BERLIN: WALL'S END

Everyone has seen the pictures of joyful celebration in West Berlin, the vast crowds stopping the traffic on the Kurfurstendamm, *Sekt* corks popping, strangers tearfully embracing—the greatest street party in the history of the world. Yes, it was like that. But it was not only like that. Most of the estimated two million East Germans who flooded into West Berlin over the weekend simply walked the streets in quiet family groups, often with toddlers in pushchairs. They queued up at a bank to collect the 100 Deutschmarks "greeting money" offered to visiting East Germans by the West German government, and then they went, very cautiously, shopping. Generally they bought one or two small items, perhaps some fresh fruit, a Western newspaper and toys for the children. Then, clasping their carrier-bags, they walked quietly back through the Wall, through the gray, deserted streets of East Berlin, home.

It is very difficult to describe the quality of this experience because what they actually did was so stunningly ordinary. In effect, they just took a bus and went shopping in the West End. Berliners walked the streets of Berlin. What could be more normal? And yet, what could be more fantastic! "Twenty-eight years and ninety-one days," says one man in his late thirties strolling back up Friedrichstrasse. Twenty-eight years and ninety-one days, since the building of the Wall. On that day, in August 1961, his parents had wanted to go to a late-night Western in the Western cinema, but their eleven-year-old son had been too tired. In the early hours they woke to the sound of tanks. He had never been to West Berlin from that day to this. A taxi driver asks me, with a sly smile: "How much is the ferry to England?" The day before yesterday his question would have been unthinkable.

But everyone is inwardly changed, changed utterly. "Now people are standing up straight," says a hotel porter. "They are speaking their minds. Even work is more fun. I think the sick will get up from their hospital beds." And it was in East rather than West Berlin that this weekend had the magic, Pentecostal quality which I last experienced in Poland in autumn 1980. Ordinary men and women find their voice and their courage—*Lebensmut,* as the porter puts it. These are moments when you feel that somewhere an angel has opened his wings.

They may have been ordinary people doing very ordinary things, but the Berliners immediately grasped the historical dimensions of the event. "Of course the real villain was Hitler," said one. A note stuck to a remnant of the Wall read: "Stalin is dead, Europe lives." The man who counted twenty-eight years and ninety-one days told me he had been most moved by an improvised poster saying: "Only today is the war really over."

As soon as the Hungarians started cutting the barbed wire of the "iron curtain," in May, East Germans began to escape across it. As the numbers grew, and East Germans gathered in refugee camps in Budapest, the Hungarian authorities decided, in early September, to let them leave officially (suspending a bilateral

(Continues on p. 82)

1989?
Péter Pócs
Hungary, 1989

When the East Germans
began a mass exodus across
the Hungarian border in fall
1989, Pócs replaced the
communist insignia on the
GDR flag with a suitcase.

consular agreement with East Germany). The trickle turned into a flood: some 15,000 crossed the border in the first three days, 50,000 by the end of October. Others sought an exit route via the West German embassies in Prague and Warsaw. This was the final catalyst for internal change in East Germany.

Yet the opening of the Berlin Wall on November 9, and subsequently of the whole inter-German frontier, changed the terms of the revolution completely. Before November 9, the issue had been how this state—the German Democratic Republic—should be governed. The people were reclaiming their so-called people's state. They were putting the D for Democratic into the GDR. After November 9, the issue was whether this state should continue to exist at all.

I witnessed this moment of change at the epicenter of the revolution, in Leipzig, on a bitterly cold Monday evening twelve days after the opening of the Wall. Through freezing mist I found my way to the packed Church of St. Nicholas. Inside, the homily was about Cain and Abel. People like Cain should not be allowed to carry on in power, said the preacher. But they should have the chance to live on, to make amends. The theme of the whole service was the need for understanding, tolerance, reconciliation. Yet there was not too much of that spirit on display in the vast crowd outside, on and around Karl-Marx-Platz. Placards showed Erich Honecker in prison uniform and behind bars. Speaker after speaker denounced forty years of lies, corruption, privilege, and waste.

A source of palpable fascination was the rulers' alleged abuse of hard-currency transfers from West Germany. "Where has all the currency gone?" people sang, to the tune of "Where have all the flowers gone?" And one speaker answered, to rapturous applause, with fantastic tales of how the party leaders had bought themselves a whole island in the Caribbean, and how Margot Honecker, the former education minister and wife of Erich Honecker, used to fly to Paris every month for a hairdo. ... Everyone agreed on two immediate central demands: free elections and an end to the party's *Führungsanspruch*—its "leadership claim."

"Socialism has not delivered what it promised," another speaker asserted, and the promised "new socialism" would not deliver it either. Loud applause. "We are not laboratory rabbits." They had waited and labored long enough. They all know that a free-market economy works. "Our compatriots in the Federal Republic are not foreigners." There should therefore, he said, be a referendum on reunification. At this point a small group started chanting the slogan that was already painted on several banners: *Deutschland, einig Vaterland!* "Germany, united fatherland" (words from the East German "national" anthem that caused Honecker to order that the anthem should never be sung, only the music played). The vast crowd quickly took up the chant: *Deutschland, einig Vaterland!* they roared, "DEUTSCHLAND, EINIG VATERLAND!" And I had to pinch myself to make sure that I was not dreaming, that I really was standing on Karl-Marx-Platz, in Leipzig, in the middle of East Germany, while a hundred thousand voices cried, "Germany, united fatherland!"

In this crowd it must be said, almost every conceivable tendency (except

(Continues on p. 84)

Hero City
Feliks Büttner
East Germany, 1990

This poster commemorates
the mass demonstrations in
Leipzig during the fall of
1989, key to bringing down
the East German party and
state.

communism) was represented. Green banners were raised behind those demanding reunification, a placard saying "Free Farmers" was hoisted beside a blue-and-gold European Community flag. Yet one already felt, instinctively, that the voices for reunification were the voices that would prevail. Not because of the power of nationalism. Just because of the power of common sense. The alternatives offered by the fledgling opposition groups, whether New Forum, the SDP, "Democratic Awakening," or "Democracy Now," were so vague, inchoate, uncertain. The alternative offered by West Germany was just so immediately, so obviously, so overwhelmingly plausible. "Mercedes! Buy the Sachsenring factory!" demanded another banner at the front of the crowd. The frontiers were open. The people had seen West Germany—and it worked.

There was the growing number of people who simply voted for reunification with their feet, by emigrating to West Germany: some 2,000 a day in January 1990, the same number that had originally precipitated the building of the Wall in August 1961. And then there were innumerable examples of practical cooperation and joint enterprise across the inter-German frontier and through the Wall: new air links, bus routes, joint ventures.

This was most dramatically visible in Berlin. Where previously a West Berlin underground line ran through ghostly, sealed underground stations in East Berlin, the doors of the train now opened and East Berliners leapt aboard. The whole mental geography of Berlin changed overnight. What had been the edge became the center. It was one city again. But it was also true all around the German-German borders. Unification was happening from below. It happened because many people on both sides wanted it to happen.

As I write, in January 1990, the euphoria of October and November has already turned into consternation and alarm—both in Germany and among her partners and neighbors, to East and West. It seems all the more important to recall that original moment of hope and joy. The moment when people who for years had been silenced could at last speak their minds; when people were free at last to travel, who for years had been locked in. It was a moment of emancipation and liberation, created by the people of East Germany. They had waited as long as the other peoples of East Central Europe for this moment, and they had as much right to it as any other people.

TIMOTHY GARTON ASH
The Magic Lantern, 1990

Neid !
Erkanneinfachalles.

Envy! The Half-Hearted One
GRAPPA
East Germany, 1989

A group of artists called GRAPPA ridicules East German leader Egon Krenz, who replaced Erich Honecker in October 1989 and completely failed to stem the revolutionary tide.

YOU HAVE BUILT ME A HOUSE

you have built me a house
let me begin another

you have placed a chair for me
now put dolls in your lounge chair

you have saved money for me
I would rather steal

you have opened a road for me
I'll slash my way
through shrubs at the side of the road

should you say
go alone
I would go
with you

WOLFGANG HILBIG
East Germany

1940
Gunárs Lusis
Latvia, 1989

The Communist star rises
and sets in Latvia's dark
night.

CONTENTION AND FRICTION

Contention and friction are less evident from without than they are from within; thus, dramatic changes viewed from the outside are somewhat more surprising than when they are experienced from the inside.

This is not to say that someone on the inside could have foreseen November 1989 in Czechoslovakia in its full historic significance: politically active dissidents did not suppose that the power of the state, i.e., of the Party, was so undermined and indecisive in its visible presence; the Party did not suppose, even in its reform wing, that intellectual dissent would be so adept at decision-making and organization. A chess game was in progress, in which the red blacks simply failed to spot the free white pawn on square D 7, which moved irrevocably on to become a queen. Its name was Václav Havel.

When state security officer Zivčák, disguised as student Růžička, led the mainly student processsion on November 17 from Vyšehrad to National Avenue, where a planned police intervention waited in white helmets, ready to move against those pressed between the cordon and the barbed-wire vehicles—he supposed that he was serving the new Party clique. Or the KGB. Or *perestroika*. Acting upon this supposition, he played dead, and Czech streets aren't quite as clean as they might be.

The students and young people in the procession knew it was important to be there, it was a chance to have a go at something reasonable after forty years of feeble-minded rule. They did not guess that a cynical ambush awaited them, and a species of frenzied young policeman, who would boldly sally out at his victim, hammer away with his truncheon and dash back into the cordon. Or stand alongside the one narrow passage, down which people had to run in single file, hammering and hammering away, though he was a Czech or Slovak too, as well as a human being with some kind of a mind.

> *Imagination*
> Mitts off your head, you bloody swine,
> he said,
> then hit her with his truncheon.
>
> What stirred the imagination
> of this armed man, until
> the flowers the girls were holding
> seemed to him, under his standing orders,
> like an assassination attempt on Lenin,
> and the candles like booby-trapped bombs?
>
> Maybe too long a sojourn
> in a landscape without any shade,

(Continues on p. 90)

**Czechoslovak Autumn
1989**
*Radomír Postl
Czechoslovakia, 1989*

A poster created for an
exhibition of photographs
about the "Velvet Revolu-
tion."

where stones sweat blood in daytime
and at night foul water
devalues the moon in wavelets. Where
the jaws of a circled snake
swallow the snake's tail,
abortion equals rebirth,
on a separate planet, where
behind the screen of tear gas
you can barter Beria's three golden hairs
for a couple of quarters. Where slaughterhouse
cattle moo at the Marseillaise
and skulls dissolve while
cyanide salts are formed. Where rules
the black frost of rum.

What stirred the imagination
of the boy who wanted
a tall ship and a star
to steer her by?

And what's left behind on the ground
is a reddish puddle
with her blood
and his dream
of ship and star,
coagulating.

On National Avenue on November 18th, there remained scraps of clothing, caps, scarves, and blood on the walls. People began to place candles there, as they had done for the past twenty years on Jan Palach's grave, even though Palach had been cremated a second time over and removed, and a certain Mrs. Jedličková was buried there instead, chosen because she had no relatives. All of us know that Marie Jedličková is Jan Palach, just as Genghis Khan or Louis XIV is either Stalin or Brezhnev.

On the 19th, an elderly lady lighting a candle on National Avenue was given a supplementary beating by a policeman, famed for calling across to the police van: "Hey you, hurry up and gimme that truncheon."

That was the last authentic sentence of a regime that began forty-one years earlier in Prague, declaring they would follow the Soviet Union for Ever and Ever without Fail.

A regime, which suffered basic damage from within in 1968, when Alexander Dubček's Czechoslovakia opposed overweening autocracy with a rational program for adjusting human affairs, still under the socialist label, a time rife with the

(Continues on p. 92)

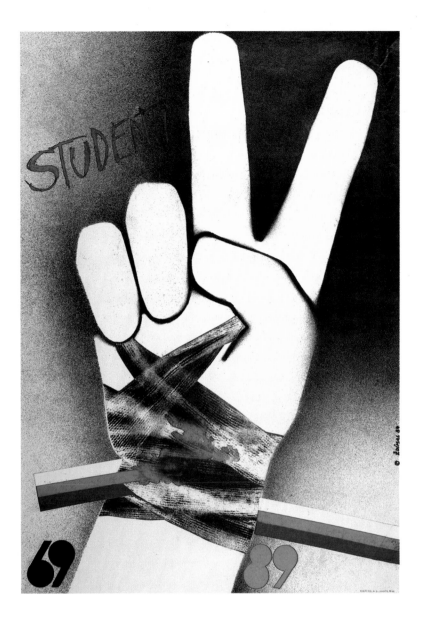

Students
Dušan Ždímal
Czechoslovakia, 1989
Lent by Dana Bartelt

The artist remembers
unarmed students injured
during clashes with armed
police in Czechoslovakia
during the 1968–69
demonstrations and the
1989 "Velvet Revolution."

blooming atherosclerosis and paranoia of the Russian generals and Leonid Brezhnev, and long before the ascension to the Kremlin of Mikhail Gorbachev.

A regime, basically and definitively undermined by the intervention of Soviet tanks in August 1968, after which belonging to the Communist Party in Czechoslovakia was like having venereal disease.

The damage of 1968 and the ensuing years completed the process of divorce between word and fact, the language of communication was dissolved and the language of mimicry installed in its place. People were displaced by cardboard cut-outs or colored camouflage, and knew they had been displaced, many even in their own souls. This divorce and displacement was experienced so strongly, that at the first possible opportunity practically everyone went out into the streets on a quest of self-rediscovery.

Twenty-four hours later Prague was plastered, not only with declarations of institutions and individuals, and slogans and cartoons opposing police terror, but also quotations from T. G. Masaryk, Marcus Aurelius, Nietzsche, Karel Čapek, Rabindranath Tagore, and—notably—Gandhi too, for it was not a matter of violence, but of revolt against "being just like them." An incredible number of anonymous people covered the walls with their own thoughts and poems— thereby supplying an unusually solid argument in favor of poetry. Overnight the walls of Prague and Czechoslovakia became a source of communication and even rather fine documentary writing.

> *The Third Language*
> It was empty
> inside the head
> and speechless.
> People were neutralized
> by statutory people.
>
> And so it happened
> that something like a disinherited idea
> thought people up.
>
> People from holes, people from houses,
> people from cold storage, people from fly ash,
> people from hot water,
> *people from the conflagration of trees.*
>
> *And suddenly they were one flash.*
> And suddenly it was Josef Hora's
> *at last.*

(Continues on p. 94)

Charter 77
Václav Ševčík
Czechoslovakia, 1977

Prague intellectuals produced "Charter 77," a document calling on the government to respect human rights as international treaties they signed obligated them to do. The yellow sun symbolizes a brighter future, which is ominously encircled by the tread marks of tanks.

People
came from everywhere, gathered,
went one way, equal to themselves,
identified with one another,
like stem cells from the bone marrow
of the idea.
The idea thought up people
with three hands, people
with three colors above the gray dirt,
people with three languages,
Czech, Slovak,
and another one.

An uproar rose over the heads.
to the heavy, overcast sky.
It had no words.
It couldn't be bugged.
But they all understood.

The dictionary of the third language
lay in the square
and the newborn wind
was leafing through it. In this language
oxygen is oxygen
and a conic section passes through a fixed point
and intersects a fixed line.

A statutory man
in a Mercedes with a special license plate
left without deciphering
the code of the third language.
He was silent.

Because too many people
for the first time in life
were really speaking.

Fortunately, thanks to organized dissent and people of Václav Havel's caliber, matters did not rest with this Third Language, but went on to the organization of a Third Democratic Czechoslovak Republic. In the process of organization much of the poetry and words got lost in the muck, but the facts remained, along with a certain number of people who know that the Czechoslovak model of the fight for survival is much the same as the worldwide problem—or, for great optimists, the model of how to live.

MIROSLAV HOLUB
Czechoslovakia, 1991

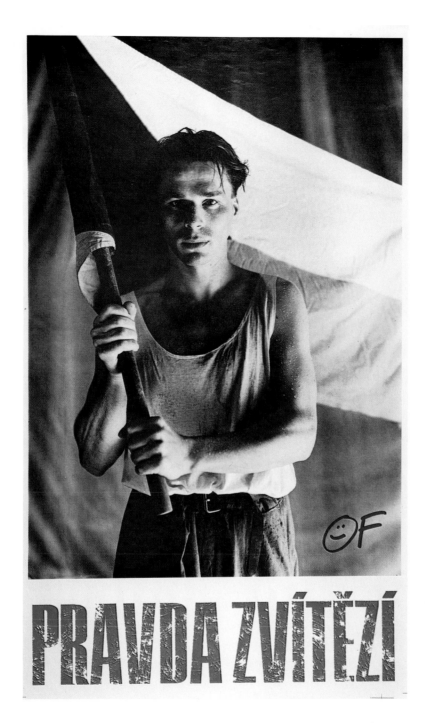

Truth Is Victorious
Václav Jírasek & Bratrstvo
Czechoslovakia, 1989
Lent by Dana Bartelt

Members of the rock group
Bratrstvo ("Brotherhood")
produced this poster. "OF"
stands for Civic Forum, the
victorious democratic
movement led by Václav
Havel.

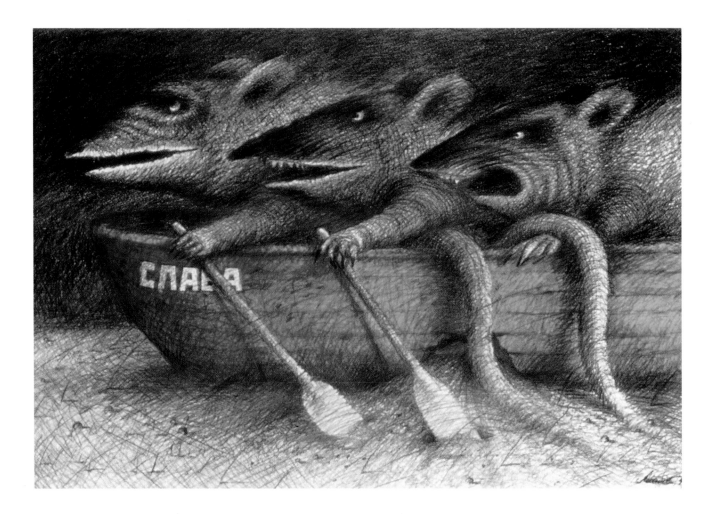

right:

Hoorah!
Alexander Chantsev
Russia, 1989

Chantsev depicts the "red rats" as the first to jump ship and take the lifeboat, but their oars are stuck in the dirt—they're going nowhere. "Hoorah!" is the parade cheer of the Communist party.

Untitled
Anonymous
Czechoslovakia, 1989
Gouache

A modern Pied Piper leads the "red rats" out of town.

From the
LETTER OF LIVING CHAINS

Now there is a process taking place, they say and write on walls, students, that it is a velvet revolution . . . . The Hungarians began it and the Polish began it, and before us the East Germans got into it and tore down the wall . . . changing Central Europe is already here and Wałeşa is here with his Solidarity and . . . Prague and other cities are now joined by a living chain of human hands, in which there are flowers and lighted candles, crowds of thousands and hundreds of thousands in the squares . . . students and those who are forming a new society, a new way of being and living. . . . Students who were also beaten November 17th by police, and, it makes no difference whether in white helmets or red berets, but, beaten so that they suffered not only serious injuries, but also psychic shocks like the ones remembered by those who live through air raid attacks and times in concentration camps. . . . and yet they did not surrender. Prague is now one big beehive, all the streets and metro walls are covered with posters, every poster an original, students make up new slogans as the situation changes every hour, new appeals and proclamations . . . students surmise the political and humanitarian situation and post on walls their short essays . . . and so in the heart of Europe literature originates, a new kind of creative art, new comics, new engaged pop art and the theaters are closed and yet opened where meetings are held and new songs sung and people who had to emigrate into themselves or really emigrate appear on the stage . . . and join the new Prague Spring, even though it is November and frosty.

BOHUMIL HRABAL
Czechoslovakia, December 8, 1989

Fall 89/Spring 68
Aleš Najbrt
Czechoslovakia, 1989
Silkscreen

Positioned as shown this poster reminds the viewer of the Prague Spring; inverted, the poster reads "Fall 89," the time of the revolution.

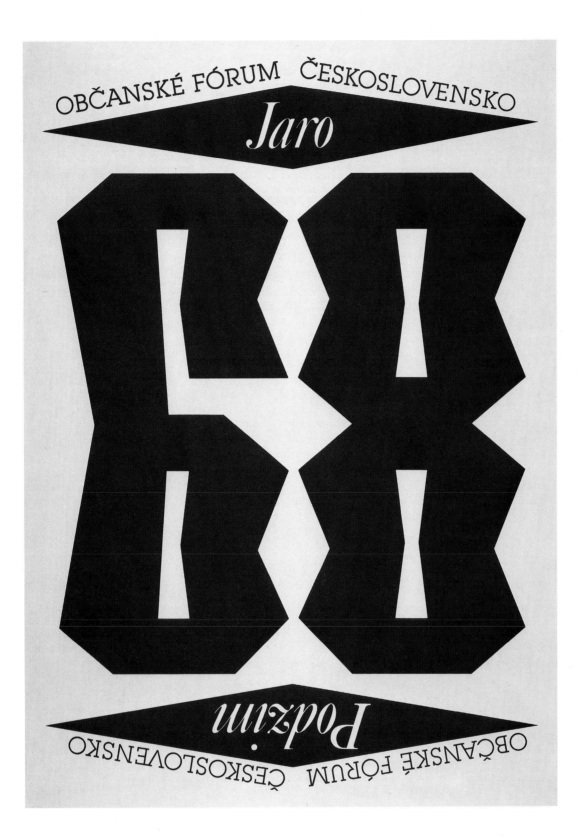

OBČANSKÉ FÓRUM   ČESKOSLOVENSKO

Jaro

88

Podzim

OBČANSKÉ FÓRUM   ČESKOSLOVENSKO

KEEPING CALM IN PRAGUE

Not so long ago, the powers that be silenced him and locked him up from time to time. Now Havel is in the Castle. Over there, the Castle, rising above Prague, and in it the man whom the people of Prague have accepted in their hearts as their spokesman.

Myth and magic are of primary importance, and the Czech writer who goes home weekends to write his next speech since he wants to read his own text, and who truly writes what he thinks, has become the symbol of Central European non-violent democratic change that initiates us as authentic citizens of this ancient continent, granting us our own individuality in our own home.

Havel has particular dreams these days: He sits on a prison bunk and tells his cell-mates that, to be sure, he used to be the president. They shake their heads, laugh, and point their index fingers at their foreheads: "What is it, Vasek [Václav], has the clink affected your brain?"

GEORGE KONRÁD
Hungary

HAVEL NA HRAD

HAVEL NA HRADĚ!

Havel to the Castle
Havel's in the Castle
Joska Skalník
Czechoslovakia, 1989
Photo by Miloš Fikejz
(Havel's in the Castle *lent by*
Dana Bartelt)

An anonymous addition of
an "ě" changed the meaning
of this poster.

THE STATE OF THE EMPIRE

The first pictures of the Prague demonstration of November 17th were of young girls placing flowers on shields held by riot police. Later the police got rough, but their furious brutality failed to provoke a single violent response. Not one car was damaged, not one window smashed during daily demonstrations by hundreds of thousands of people. Posters stuck up on the walls of houses, in metro stations, on shop windows, and in trains by striking students called for peaceful protest. Flowers became the symbol of Civic Forum.

It is only recently that we have seen the fragility of totalitarian power. Is it really possible that a few days of protest—unique in the history of revolutions for their peacefulness—could topple a regime which had harassed our citizens for four decades?

The rest of the world had all but forgotten the 1968 invasion of Czechoslovakia by the armies of five countries. Even now, our nation has barely recovered from that invasion: what did not recover was the leading force in the country, the Communist Party. By subsequently making approval of the invasion and the occupation a condition of membership, the Party deprived itself of almost all patriotic and worthy members, becoming for the rest of the nation a symbol of moral decay and betrayal.

The government, then stripped of its authority and its intelligence, went on to devastate the country culturally, morally, and materially. An economically mature country fell back among the developing countries, while achieving a notable success in atmospheric pollution, incidence of malignant tumors, and short life expectancy.

Unrestrained power breeds arrogance. And arrogance threatens not only the subject but also the ruler. In Czechoslovakia, the ruling party, deprived of an elite and of any outstanding personalities, combined arrogance with provocative stupidity. It persisted obstinately in defending the occupation of Czechoslovakia, indeed in defending the occupation of Czechoslovakia as an act of deliverance at a time when even the invaders themselves were re-examining their past.

The months leading up to the events of November, however static they may have seemed compared with the agitation in the neighboring countries, were in fact a period of waiting for circumstances to change. The regime, unable to discern its utter isolation, in relation to both its own nation and the community of nations, reacted in its usual manner to a peaceful demonstration commemorating the death of a student murdered by the Nazis fifty years ago. It could not have picked a worse moment—the patience of the silent nation had snapped; the circumstances had finally changed.

IVAN KLÍMA
Czechoslovakia

Civic Forum—Hey! Get to Work! The Garden Is Wasted, the Cesspool Is Full, and the Cottage Is About to Fall
Vladimír Renčín
Czechoslovakia, 1990

In this election poster Renčín suggests Civic Forum stop its political talk and get down to fixing Czechoslovakia's real problems.

Stalin
Jan Meisner
Czechoslovakia, 1989
Silkscreen

The artist alludes to the difficulty of understanding the Stalin phenomenon in this theater poster by depicting him as the eternally unfathomable Mona Lisa.

Unfortunately, Our Statutes Don't Know Any Other Way to Leave
Vladimír Jiránek
Czechoslovakia, 1989
Lent by Dana Bartelt

A satire of the unceremonious exit of Czechoslovak Communist leaders.

No More
Jiří Slíva
Czechoslovakia, 1989
Lent by Dana Bartelt

Bureaucrats will not be able to lean on the workers anymore, the artist says.

Transylvania
Péter Pócs
Hungary, 1988

An empty Bible with
Romanian tricolor
bookmark represents the
absence of religious freedom in Romania under
Ceauşescu's dictatorship.

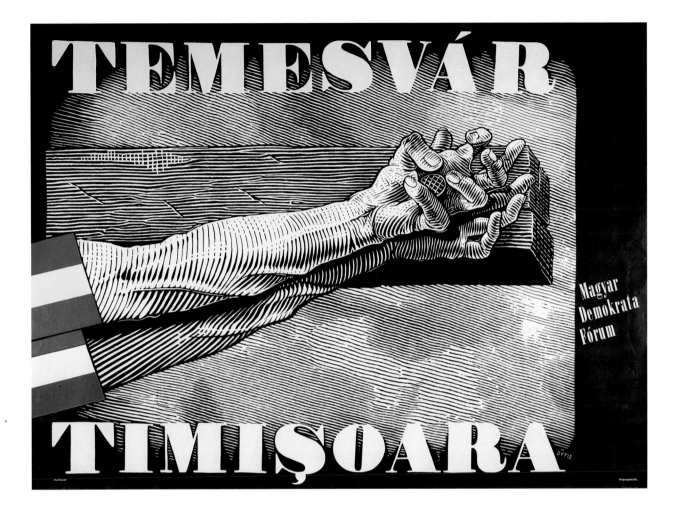

Temesvár-Timișoara
István Orosz
Hungary, 1990

In a poster for the populist ruling party, the Hungarian Democratic Forum, Orosz pays tribute to the Romanian and Hungarian victims who died during the 1989 demonstrations in the Romanian town of Timișoara.

STANDARD ISOLATION

I have been blind, blind as a mole
and I said to myself, "I'll burn all the books
in the vulgar fire of doubt, I'll feed on sweet roots,
I'll sleep with my head on a stone"
Blind as a mole by a small heap of words.
The laws cut off the germinal bulbs of error,
pump the water into endless galleries.
"Blind as a fruit"
Who will invent a language just to be alone?
"blind as a fruit, blind as a mole"
(Enthusiastic and illiterate, I loved you in African forests,
I fought with the missionary, sang late into the night,
Eros kynegethikos, Eros kynegethikos,
broke my poisoned arrows.
Then I took the books and burned them.)
But what do I see now? What can I describe when
eyes have sprouted all over my body?
An earth worm digs small, irregular galleries under my feet,
pain pushes me to the ocean, anaesthesia, mother,
I go into the water, I have burned all the books,
I grow transparent, transparent.
I see my heart within me: a happy red mole

ION MORAR
Romania

Book
Miklós Onucsan
Romania, 1990
Mixed media

The book represents the burning of the National Library in Bucharest. The two hammers symbolize the violent attacks of pro-Communist miners on the democratic opposition in June 1990.

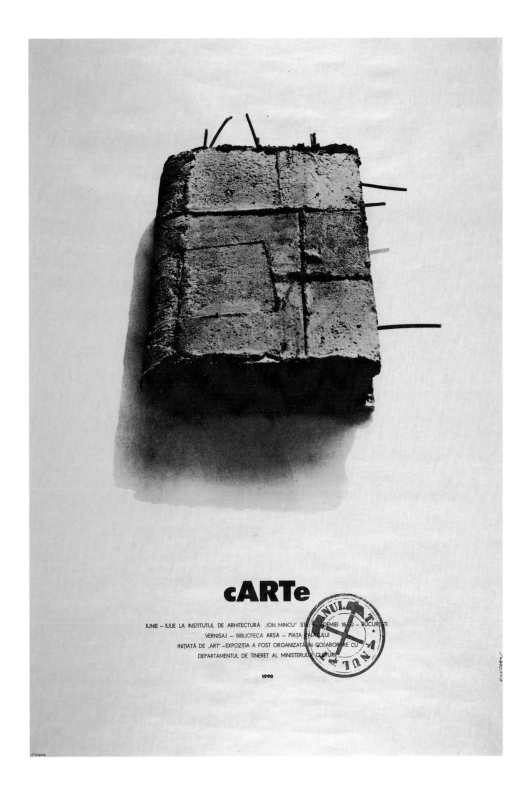

cARTe

IUNIE – IULIE LA INSTITUTUL DE ARHITECTURĂ „ION MINCU" STR. ACADEMIEI 18-20 – BUCUREȘTI
VERNISAJ – BIBLIOTECA ARSĂ – PIAȚA PALATULUI
INIȚIATĂ DE „ART" – EXPOZIȚIA A FOST ORGANIZATĂ ÎN COLABORARE CU
DEPARTAMENTUL DE TINERET AL MINISTERULUI CULTURII

1990

A CONVERSATION WITH WRITER MIRCEA DINESCU

The revolution in Romania was carried out by people in the street. In my opinion, it wasn't a revolution. It was more of a street movement. All sorts of scenarios are discussed in the West: that it was a coup of the old party activists. In my opinion, the head of the coup was Ceaușescu himself, who on December 21 had the only brillant idea of his life: to gather ten thousand hungry workers and lecture them on the high standards of living in Romania. This meeting was televised. *He* gave the signal to revolt.

The people in the provinces heard how Ceaușescu was booed, and they all ran out into the streets. Of course, after this, the old professionals of power, who had networks throughout the country, grabbed the power. In Romania there was no Charter 77 like in Czechoslovakia, no Solidarity as in Poland, there were just a few dissidents—most of them under house arrest. We were in no way organized. We didn't even know each other. We were dabs of paint in the December Movement. For the rest, the gray power was the majority—the all-pervading power.

People were highly dissatisfied. Romania had the lowest standard of living in Eastern Europe. We had a Stalinist dictatorship cum Latin American dictatorship with a bunch of family mafia. At the time Romania was very much like a time bomb, waiting for the moment to go off. During his speech on December 21, Ceaușescu somehow pressed the button. It was the starting point. The Securitate did not really expect the masses to come out into the streets. They started repressing the masses in Timișoara, then in Bucharest. What they didn't expect was that the fear, which they had carefully instilled in the population, simply melted away, and people, emptyhanded, opposed the tanks and the machine guns. Obviously, both the army and the Securitate, after the events took a clear turn, made a pact with the representatives of the new power. That's why power in Romania was grabbed by former party activists who in Ceaușescu's time had fallen into disgrace.

In retrospect, I realize that I was a romantic naïve. I thought that such a revolution, even if it lasted for three days, would change people for the better. Unfortunately, villainy increased because the former Communists became the present anti-Communists. Those who preached for the lay state now are taking part in religious processions. Writers who praised the dictatorship or kept a coward silence are now posing as dissidents. The nationalism which Ceaușescu had sown was reborn in even more disgusting and painful forms.

For forty years communism was a very organized chaos. Now we are only left with the chaos. The people organizing chaos in Ceaușescu's time became self-styled capitalists. For years we had lectures on the rotten state of capitalism. Overnight these lecturers have turned into theoreticians of market economy. They witnessed the dismantling of Lenin's statue and they cheered, though they were the ones who cheered when Lenin's statue was first raised. We're witnessing some ridiculous shows, in which a new demagogy begins to replace reality.

Interviewed by **MICHAEL MARCH**
Bucharest, 1991

Homage to Romania
Péter Pócs & László Haris
Hungary, 1989

An homage to the victims of Romania's December 1989 revolution.

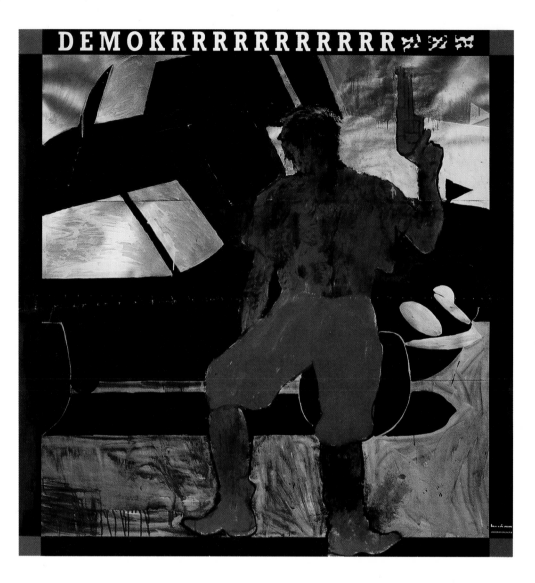

Demokrrrrrrrrrr
Boris Bućan
Yugoslavia, 1990

Taking the side of free elections in Croatia, Bućan depicts the starter's red gun in the race toward democracy.

right:

Democracy-Freedom-Peace
Boris Bućan
Yugoslavia, 1990

The artist heralds the victory of democracy with a red-and-white checkered flag, representing the traditional Croatian coat-of-arms.

THE TRANSITION

In the beginning was Koch Strasse. One fine day it was split in two by a Wall. This Wall became the emblem of postwar Europe, of all the ugliness and stupidity Europe got itself into, East and West alike, if in different ways, simply by calling itself two, by forgetting about the other half, and thus about itself.

Now the Wall has come down, a great event, a historical moment.

So, what now? Now, once again, there is Koch Strasse. A great event? Not really. Just a street, where the sun shines, the wind blows, one shop thrives, the other doesn't, there are those who feel fine, and those who whine.

In this country historical moments run thick and fast. The significance of this cannot be stressed too much. A country condemned to silence—or which chose silence—has now begun to speak. One might even say that the last forty years were spent in hiding from the madness called state socialism; bearing in mind that such hiding also involved a degree of infiltration. These forty years were not years of heroism, but of shit, shit, and more shit. Excuse the expression. We ruined this country. Today it's much easier to say: *they* ruined this country. That's understandable, but at the end of the day a country is a collective product—which means it's probably safer to say that, one way or another, the country has *been ruined.* It's perhaps inevitable that the first word of our newly found speech should belong to the naming of villains (naming, not revenge). But our second word must belong to ourselves. For the real loss of our forty years of hiding has been our failure to ask ourselves the simplest of questions: how would we like to live, what are our plans, what kind of jackets do we like, what kind of pâtés, political parties, women, men? . . . Instead, always the same cautious ducking and diving from yet another of their "new ideas" . . . Only slowly we forgot the diving, and what we might want if we no longer wanted what we wanted.

We are disillusioned, and there's no big business in disillusion. It's everyone's loss if today the word socialism crops up in a sentence only to render the whole paragraph frivolous; it's everyone's loss if communism is not some kind of eternal

(Continues on p. 116)

Make Your Choice
Sándor Kállay
Hungary, 1990
Mixed media

Campaigning for a political party with a young constituency, the artist depicts two Soviet leaders locked in a farewell embrace.

TESSÉK VÁLASZTANI

human dream, but only the petty conspiracy of murderers, madmen, and careerists. . . . It wasn't, as they say, always like this. But now it is like this, perhaps because it can't be otherwise. But it'll be good, or at least better, when it isn't like this any more. When words recover their sobriety and generosity.

Mankind does not live between historical coordinates. That's why—soberly, if a little ungratefully—I find myself less and less delighted by what even a year ago would have been the *ne plus ultra* of our every desire. Gradually I have to look at how things actually stand; okay, for forty years a magical formation hovered above us which has now come tumbling down, evaporated, disappeared, a fleeting kiss—but wait! the regime has collapsed, that's true; collapsed as if it never existed, that's not true, because the economic system as a force has not collapsed (only failed) and neither has the everyday regime of depradation—so where are we? Our novels have become historical novels.

Perhaps it's still too early to say such things. I'd best just get on with voting out the *com'nists.* . . . But when that's done I'll still be left strolling up and down an empty Koch Strasse. Keep cool, they tell me, and don't wax sentimental: this is a period of transition. And they're right.

PÉTER ESTERHÁZY
Hungary, 1990

For a Hungarian Future
Béla Aba
Hungary, 1990

An election poster for the Hungarian Democratic Forum (MDF), the populist party that won the 1990 election.

MAGYAR DEMOKRATA FÓRUM

A MAGYAR JÖVŐÉRT

F.K.: LIGETI IMRE

Croop Nyomda Kft. Felelős vezető: Mrenje Attila

The Political Trial of the Pensioner Kristály Gyula is depicted via the poster text:

Kristály
Gyula
ózdi
nyugdijas
politikai
pere

Iró,
rendező
Tényi
István
Alkotótárs
Sántha
László

MOVI
Fórum
Filmstudió
MAFILM
Balázs
Béla
Stúdió

FORUM

right:

The Political Trial of the Pensioner Kristály Gyula
Krzysztof Ducki
Hungary, 1989

A film poster that criticizes the Communist political trials of the 1950s, in which thousands were imprisoned or shot to satisfy Stalin's insistence on a purge.

Worker's Militia
Krzysztof Ducki
Hungary, 1989

Ducki warns about *Munkásörség*, the Worker's Militia, which served as the Communist party's armed force in Hungarian factories. Despite the party's promises to reform, the fangs soaking in a cup at bedside are ready to be put back in at a moment's call.

Munkásőrség

SZDSZ

THE PARADOX OF THE POLITICAL POSTER

Since the political poster thrives in times of oppression, totalitarianism, and especially during times of revolution, it would be best if the political poster did not exist. Unfortunately, the world is not so ideal, so, I'm afraid, it will have a long life.

PIOTR MŁODOŻENIEC
Artist, Poland

Wałęsa
Piotr Młodożeniec
Poland, 1990

The "*L*" and "*W*" that form Wałęsa's face are the logo of the Polish underground army that fought against occupying powers during World War II.

right:

Our Gang
Andrzej Pągowski
Poland, 1989

A theater poster depicts
Communist *apparatchiks*
(bureaucrats) characteristi-
cally shouting from high
podiums.

Solidarity-*High Noon*
Tomasz Sarnecki
Poland, 1989

Sarnecki shows *High Noon*
star Gary Cooper armed
with a ballot for Poland's
Solidarity party in a
showdown with Communist
"bandits." On June 4, 1989,
Solidarity won the first
democratic elections in
Eastern Europe since 1946.

W SAMO POŁUDNIE
4 CZERWCA 1989

Welcome, Pierre Cardin
Igor Vachitov
Russia, 1990
Lent by Plackart

The artist invites the famous French designer to go to work on Soviet working women.

Tractorul—**Young Artists' Group Exhibition**
Timotei Nádăşan
Romania, 1990
Silkscreen

This exhibition poster satirizes standard Communist symbols. "Hei-Rut," rising like smoke from the tractor (symbol of collectivization), is the hymn of the Romanian Communist Youth.

Who Are We? Where Are We Going?
Anatoli Reshetov & Viktor Cherenov
Russia, 1990
Silkscreen

The artists raise questions about Russia's future, reminiscent of the last page of Nikolai Gogol's 19th-century novel, *Dead Souls,* which asked, "Russia, where are you flying? Answer me!"

Gloria in Excelsis—Civic Forum!
Pavel Beneš
Czechoslovakia, 1989
Lent by Dana Bartelt

In 1989, Czech Christians openly celebrated their first Christmas in more than 40 years.

GLORIA IN EXCELSIS DEO

KLIDNÉ VÁNOCE S OBČANSKÝM FÓREM

**Gloria in Excelsis Deo—
Peaceful Christmas
with the Civic Forum**
*Michal Cihlar
Czechoslovakia, 1989
Lent by Dana Bartelt*

With its images of the Holy
Family, this Christmas
poster would not have
passed the censorship
committees of the past.

MORE NOTES ON THE THEME OF CHANGING PLACES

For example changing streets.
Famous memorials.
Places.
Or whole cities. Major cities.
An exchange of people worth thinking about.
Or, because simpler to realize, a change of administrations.
Every administration to rule for a certain length of time
every country on this earth.
Taking turns, so that the leader of San Marino rules the USA
at the same time as the leader of the USA rules San Marino.
Completely new dimensions in understanding peoples seem possible.
Of course institutions in the service of power to
move from country to country. To avoid complications, first
of all armed services.
And of course never parallel to the country of origin.
So that possibly for two months China will have a
Japanese police, the Soviet Army an American secret service
and a state administration from the GDR.
If this sounds too confusing it might be better to exchange
systems right away.
The planetary system.
Cosmic exchange of place has had little practice, while on earth
individuals accomplish the most astonishing exchanges.
Somebody working in one state suddenly appears as trusted
confidante in another threatened state.
In any case a visible motion is not necessary to effect a
change of residence. Many Germans managed it without making
a move in 1933 and 1945.
Finally, as a last possibility of making a change, one could
renovate. Which is how many talk themselves into thinking
something new has been effected.

LUTZ RATHENOW
East Germany

Wir sind das Volk

We Are the People
Matthias Gübig
East Germany, 1989
Silkscreen

Gübig addresses the
economic difficulties after
German reunification. The
"sheep"—"Ostis" (East
Germans)—feel consumed
by the "wolves"—"Westis"
(West Germans).

TO SUBJUGATE A SOCIETY

To subjugate a society is to reduce it to its most elementary level of subsistence. The decline in living standards, the limiting of comforts, the increased sense of threat—these are not inexplicable or absurd. They are a consequence not of wrong choices but of a policy—the policy of those wishing to consolidate their rule. A population weakened and exhausted by battling against so many obstacles—whose needs are never satisfied and desires never fulfilled—is vulnerable to manipulation and regimentation. The struggle for survival is above all an exercise that is hugely time-consuming, absorbing, and debilitating. If you create these "anti-conditions," your rule is guaranteed for a hundred years.

RYSZARD KAPUŚCIŃSKI
A Warsaw Diary, 1983

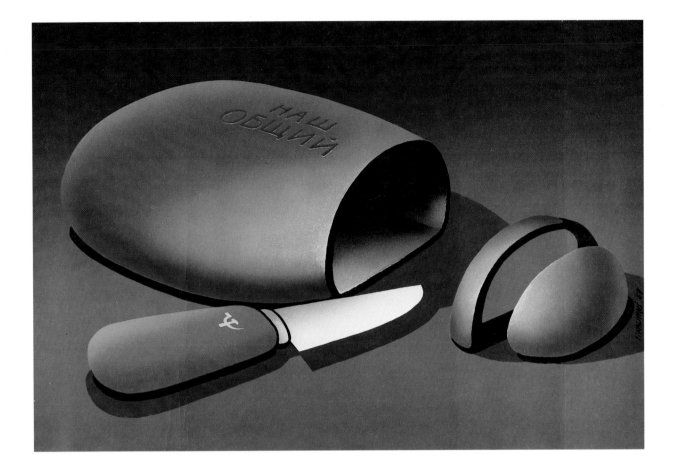

Our Daily Bread
Indulis Kalniņš
Latvia, 1989
Gouache
Lent by Plackart

A portrait of empty everyday
life in Latvia under the
Communist regime.

right:

1917
Yuri Bokser
Russia, 1989
Silkscreen

"We Want You!" a sinister
Lenin says. Only recently
have the extent of Lenin's
brutality and terror against
intellectuals and the clergy
become a matter of public
discussion in the Soviet
Union.

All the Best, Comrades
Andrei Kolosov
Russia, 1990
Silkscreen
Lent by Plackart

In the traditional style of the
icon, Kolosov alludes to the
glorification of Stalin and his
predecessor Lenin.

above right:

right:

Satyricon
Eugeniusz Get-Stankiewicz
Poland, 1990
Silkscreen

The artist evokes free Poland
with its national colors—red
and white—after the
country disposes of the
Communist red.

Socrealism
Gosha Kamenskich
Russia, 1989
Mixed media
Lent by Plackart

Kamenskich uses a prison
cup to symbolize restrictions
applied to art. For many
years socialist realism was the
only officially permitted style
in the Soviet Union.

Each Victim of State Abuse: "I'll Show It!"
Manfred Butzmann
East Germany, 1989
Lithograph

A former political prisoner,
Butzmann worked with a
human rights movement
that published cases of
violence and abuse.

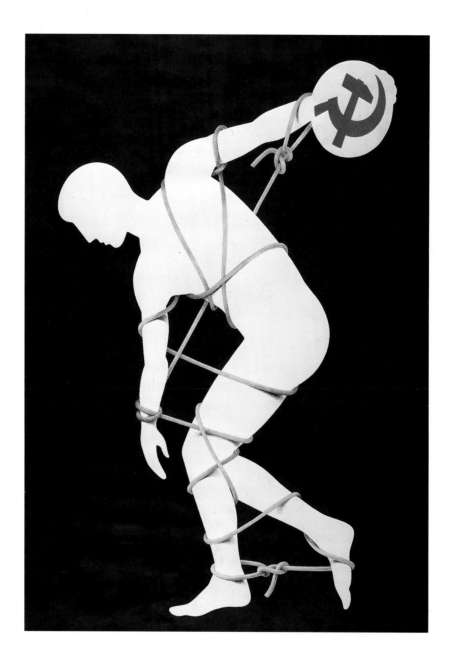

right:

Eastern European Discobolos

Károly Feleki
Romania, 1990
Gouache

With his struggling figure, Feleki suggests how difficult it is to overcome repressed economic conditions and years of mental anguish.

The "Life Blood" of Mára Zálíte

Ilmárs Blumbergs
Latvia, 1991
Silkscreen

The poet Zálíte was among the first to speak out for freedom in Eastern Europe. Her "life blood," her words, pours out to energize the youth in their fight for Latvian independence.

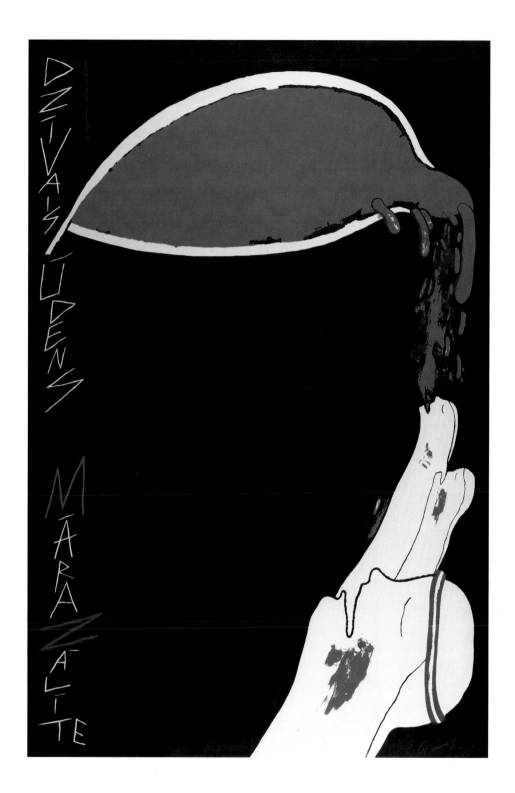

right:

Homo Soveticus
Andrei Kolosov
Russia, 1990
Silkscreen
Lent by Plackart

Leonardo da Vinci's ideal
human body is transformed
into the ideal Bolshevik.

**Great Ideas Also Have
Their Fates**
Tatyana Nyemkova
Russia, 1990
Mixed media
Lent by Plackart

In response to the Karl Marx
quote "Great Ideas Also
Have Their Fates," swarm-
ing flies form the Commu-
nist founder's portrait.

HABENT SUA FATA LIBELLI | НО И ВЕЛИКИЕ ИДЕИ ТАКЖЕ
/КНИГИ ИМЕЮТ СВОЮ СУДЬБУ./ | ИМЕЮТ СВОЮ «FATA»   К. МАРКС

A FEAST OF FREE SOULS

One of the most absurd axioms that had been inculcated into our minds since earliest childhood was: Communism is eternal. Two years ago it did seem eternal. The barbed wire and the harsh faces of the soldiers guarding the "socialist camp" were not merely pictures that I had seen in films. Barbed wire had encircled my childhood and had grown together with me.

In the fall of 1989, eighty-year-old Bulgarian dictator Zhivkov tumbled from his throne. We Bulgarians opened the windows, went out into the streets and filled the public squares. Then, at that very moment, we realized that we were many. We were as happy as children—after Poland, Hungary, Czechoslovakia, and East Germany, it was our turn.

Sofia rejoiced. Suddenly, the spacious squares of the ancient city seemed too small. So many people flocked to the Aleksander Nevski Cathedral that many had to cling to tree boughs or gather on the roofs of surrounding buildings to be witnesses of the changing times. They waved blue flags and embraced each other in joy. Communism was being effaced from the signs in the streets, from the cold marble mausoleum, from the newspaper columns. Drop by drop, as Chekov had once put it, we were squeezing the slave out of ourselves. We were squeezing the fear that had accumulated for years out of our souls. Like angry wasps, suppressed and humiliated people now started going out of their small apartments and basements. Blue flags flapped above our heads, but before our eyes flashed the ghosts of green tanks on the backs of which communism came to Eastern Europe.

In Sofia's Festival Hall, for years the Communists had held their congresses outlining Bulgaria's road to the abyss. In the spring of 1990 the Union of Democratic Forces organized a grand poetry reading in the very same hall. Never before have I seen a more enthusiastic audience. The people came to listen with waving flags in their hands. It was more than a poetry reading. It was a feast of free souls—one of those rare moments when human beings realize the power that lies within the freely spoken word. Such moments are unforgettable.

The end of communism resembles its beginning. There is the same fear, hunger, and hopelessness. But this is its end. The Communists in Russia had been dead set on making the river Ob flow backward. It did not. Neither will history.

Having been silent for so many years, we who lived to see liberation come to Eastern Europe are shouting "Freedom" and "Democracy" on the streets and in the city squares. When we stop for a while, just to catch our breath, we hear our children shouting in the silence. The red night is over, and these little roosters, in their husky voices, are announcing it to the world.

LYUBOMIR NIKOLOV
Bulgaria, 1991

Budapest 1956, Prague 1968, Vilnius 1991

Konstantin Geraymovich
Russia, 1991
Mixed media
Lent by Plackart

After Soviet gunfire killed 15 young Lithuanians on Jan. 12, 1991, a Russian artist made this poster to support Lithuanian independence.

ВЛАСТЬ

right:

Power

Alexander Chantsev
Russia, 1990
Mixed media
Lent by Plackart

Chantsev memorializes the millions terrorized and murdered during Communist rule with a red KKK-type hood.

Beware of Them

Petr Miklícek
Czechoslovakia, 1989
Drawing

After the collapse of Czechoslovakia's Communist regime, many card-carrying party members immediately "changed coats," donning tricolor ribbons and claiming to be Civic Forum supporters.

THE BITTEREST DAYS

The bitterest days for Lithuania came at the beginning of January 1991. After Moscow's ultimatums and threats, the relations between the governments of Lithuania and the USSR had become so tense that open warfare seemed imminent. In response to the prompting and support of the Kremlin, the "fifth column" infiltrated the streets. While they were not very numerous, their demands were insolent. An anonymous Committee for the Salvation of Lithuania-Kremlin front was organized. But Moscow gained nothing by these maneuvers.

Late in the night of January 12th, the unarmed citizens who were guarding the radio and TV stations were routed by Soviet fire and were crushed by the caterpillar treads of their tanks. Fifteen people died, hundreds were injured.

Vilnius was left without its main sources of information, cut off from radio, TV, and newspapers. Crowds of people journeyed from all over Lithuania, from neighboring as well as distant republics of the USSR, and surrounded the Parliament to protect it day and night. Barricades were erected. Anti-tank ditches were dug.

The walls of the Parliament House and the piled-up barricades produced a spontaneous gallery for anti-totalitarian art. All Lithuanians suddenly turned into artists—children brought their revolutionary drawings as well as toy tanks; adults displayed their medals and government certificates of merit, documents attesting Soviet citizenship, portraits of the Kremlin leaders, propaganda books, and military paraphernalia. These discarded artifacts, along with political posters, created an unforgettable impression. Menacing voices blared over the loudspeakers announcing the advance of Soviet troops, interrupted by direct transmissions from the Parliament in session, and the continuous chants of the crowd. The new poster of Lithuania, born from these events, will continue calling to its people.

JUAZOS GALKUS
Artist, Lithuania

Untitled
Vaida Knabikaite
Lithuania, 1991
Poster paint

An example of the many drawings Vilnius's children mounted on barbed wire and barricades surrounding the Lithuanian Parliament building on the night of Jan. 14, 1991.

SCRAP

After us there will be
Neither scrap metal
Nor laughter
From start to finish
We held no illusions
All our uprisings
Lie packed in the hall
With a toothbrush
and a towel

When someone knocks on the door
The echo pounds
Through the solitary years
But there is no call to action
No convoy to Siberia
Only the upstairs neighbor whose sink
Once again has overflowed
Comes wringing his hands to warn us

TOMASZ JASTRUN
Poland

Forefather's Eve
Eugeniusz Get-Stankiewicz
Poland, 1987

Adam Mickiewicz's 19th-century play, *Forefather's Eve,* concerns the Polish fight against Russian oppression. Poles consider it an artistic treasure. In 1968, the Polish regime banned it, leading to social unrest and a crackdown known as "the March days."

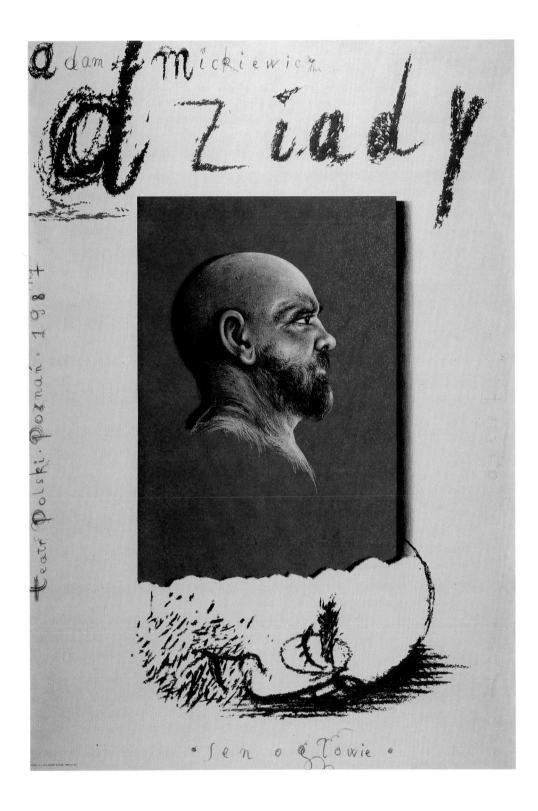

RENAMING THE PAST

"The words 'soviet' and 'socialist' are rapidly becoming obsolete in the USSR, so the letter 'S' is to be dropped from the name of our country, and soon we won't know what country we live in," writes my father in his recent letter. He still lives in Moscow, while I spend my sixteenth year far away from my native city in voluntary exile in London; but Moscow is becoming unrecognizable to both of us.

The obliteration of familiar features began with the gradual disappearance of the portraits of the Politburo members and Communist slogans from Moscow streets a few years ago. Then the pre-Revolutionary names were restored to the streets, thus making hundreds of pages of Soviet classics obsolete. Recently, in seven days, seventy years of Soviet history were obliterated; as a result, thousands of thinkers and writers have become morally unemployed. Befuddled Soviet citizens feel as if the motherland has slipped from under their feet, and they have become *émigrés* in a geography distorted by tricks of history.

The immediate past, like incriminating evidence, is threatening to everyone, because no one is unscathed. Which brain remained free of fear of KGB founder, Felix Dzerzhinsky, whose forceful personality was indelibly imprinted in the mind of every schoolboy by Soviet educationalists? An excited crowd gathered in Dzerzhinsky Square to remove his statue cheerfully and to put a noose around his bronze neck, but who would be able to rub his image out of everyone's head? The same could be said about innumerable effigies of Lenin and Marx all over the country. The image of Stalin is already engraved forever in our hearts. Having demolished the idols of the past, whom are the revolutionaries going to set on the vacant pedestals?

Having yet to shed the old Soviet identity, and already disillusioned with their grim present, people start searching their past for aristocratic ancestors; they also attempt to renew connections with relatives and former friends abroad. Old speech, with its outdated party jargon and Marxist gobbledegook, was recently crossbred with new slang of "Russified" English exported from the West by Soviet visitors abroad. Conversations in Moscow apartments have begun to resemble those in a tourist information center, with broken English barked at you from every corner. The rush for imported Western junk and pop culture comes hand in hand with a longing for pre-Revolutionary Slavic kitsch, with the Old Cyrillic everywhere on restaurants' signs, embroidered Cossack capes in old-fashioned ballrooms, and Sunday preaching among the newly converted.

These tendencies, ridiculous as they seem, prompt a crucial question: What do we face nowadays in Russia? Doesn't it look like a restoration rather than a revolution? Indeed, some of my Moscow friends do fear that this image of a kitschy traditional Russia, with compulsory religious orthodoxy and divine rights of the tsars, is replacing, as an ideal, the former vision of the Communist utopia. A Soviet habit of rewriting history according to today's ideological necessities was once encapsulated in an old joke: "We never know what's going to happen yesterday." That "yesterday" remains as mysterious as ever.

ZINOVY ZINIK
London, 1991

Comrades, Adieu!
István Orosz
Hungary, 1989

Orosz bids *adieu* to the occupying Soviet Army as it leaves Hungary.

Hungarian demonstrators,
Budapest, Spring 1989. Photo
by László Haris.

"Comrades Adieu!"
The Rise and Fall of Soviet Influence in Central and Eastern Europe, 1914–1991

GALE STOKES

Professor of History
Rice University

1914–1918
World War I

The confusion and destruction of international war weakens the Russian Empire; Bolsheviks seize power in 1917. The collapse of German and Austrian Empires permits the emergence of independent new states in Eastern Europe, including Latvia, Lithuania, and Estonia.

1918–1939
Between Two World Wars

Bolsheviks consolidate power in Soviet Union, and when Lenin dies in 1924, Stalin emerges as supreme leader. During 1930s, he collectivizes agriculture at expense of millions of peasant lives, and ruthlessly purges the party and military of most of its original, "old guard" leadership. In Eastern Europe, the new nation states prove contentious, economically weak, and, by the end of the 1930s, easy prey to economic domination by Hitler's Germany.

1939–1945
World War II

Arch ideological enemies Hitler and Stalin become allies in August 1939, leaving Hitler free to invade Poland on September 1. Two weeks later, Soviets invade from the other direction and seize eastern Poland, deporting one and a half million Poles to Siberia. In 1940, Soviets invade and annex Bessarabia (Moldavia) and Baltic states, and deport tens of thousands. In 1941, Hitler turns on Soviet Union, invading in force. With enormous loss of life, Soviets turn the tide in 1943. In 1945, Stalin's Red Army sweeps through Eastern Europe to Berlin. Soviet Union keeps eastern Poland, and Poland receives in return German lands up to Oder-Neisse line.

1945–1948
Stalinization of Eastern Europe

Seeking a protective shield around Soviet Union, Stalin imposes Communist rule on every East European state, disregarding Yalta agreements that called for democratic elections. Yalta becomes a symbol to East Europeans of their abandonment by West.

1948–1953
The Early Cold War

Stalin's puppet governments in Eastern Europe completely destroy the pre-war economic and social structures of their countries and impose rigid authoritarian regimes. United States reacts with the Marshall Plan of aid to Western Europe and policy of containment.

1948

Yugoslavia, a staunch ally of Stalin, is ejected from commonwealth of fraternal socialist states because Stalin cannot abide independent attitude of Tito's national revolution. Yugoslavia experiments with workers' self-management, its own road to socialism. Border barriers are established between socialist states and neighboring Western countries. Eastern European countries greatly restrict the foreign travel of their citizens.

1949

Unable to reach agreement on peace treaty for Germany, the Western powers (United States, Great Britain, and France) assist in the creation of German Federal Republic (West Germany); Soviets create German Democratic Republic (East Germany).

1953

Stalin dies. From this point on, history of Central and Eastern Europe concerns the question of how to protect, reform, or abandon Stalinism. In Soviet Union, a brief thaw ensues under leadership of Nikita Khrushchev. In East Germany, uprising workers are put down with armed force.

1956

June–October

Outbreak of rioting in Poznań leads to end of Stalinist leadership in Poland and installation of national Communist Władisław Gomułka.

October–November

Reaction to events in Poland leads to Hungarian Revolution, which Soviets brutally repress. Imre Nagy, reform Communist who leads the revolution, is abducted, shot, and buried in an unmarked grave. His martyrdom becomes potent focus of anti-Soviet sentiment.

1957

Soviets launch the first artificial earth satellite. Sputnik's beep-beep signal galvanizes a nervous West.

Student demonstrator faces police in Prague, Nov. 17, 1989. Photo by Jan Šibík.

1961

East Germany builds a wall through city of Berlin to prevent mass emigration of its citizens into West Germany.

1961–62

Soviet Union and China contest leadership of international Communist movement. Romania uses controversy to establish an independent foreign policy. During 1960s, West realizes the Communist movement is polycentric rather than monolithic.

1964

Leonid Brezhnev replaces Khrushchev and permits a brief flirtation with economic reform, which comes to a complete end by 1969. Brezhnev and his ruling elite remain in power until 1982, a period now called "the era of stagnation."

1968

Encouraged by modest reforms in Soviet Union, East Europeans in intellectual and economic circles write prolifically in the 1960s about how to change Stalinism into socialism with a human face. In Poland, student unrest over showing of mildly anti-Russian play *Forefather's Eve* leads to a demonstration, a purging of the party, and repression of intellectuals. Workers don't protest. In Czechoslovakia, efforts to reform communism under leadership of Alexander Dubček induce Warsaw Pact forces to invade Czechoslovakia on August 21, thus quelling "the Prague Spring." In the "Brezhnev doctrine," the Soviet leader announces that his country will intervene to maintain any socialist state. Economic and political re-

forms in Central and Eastern Europe are put on hold. New Czechoslovak leader Gustáv Husák pursues a policy of "normalization," which means strict social control. Czech and Slovak intellectuals are uprooted and placed in service jobs, such as window washers and boiler tenders.

1969

January 16

Jan Palach, a Czech student, burns himself to death in Wenceslas Square, becoming a symbol and martyr for democratic opposition in Czechoslovakia.

October

Social Democrats take power in West Germany under leadership of Willy Brandt, who introduces "Ostpolitik." Policy leads to international recognition of East Germany and closer economic ties between the two Germanies.

December 1970–January 1971

Riots over price increases in Poland lead to replacement of Gomułka by Edward Gierek, who promises new social contract: work harder for higher standard of living.

1975

Thirty-five countries sign Helsinki Agreements that were sought originally by Soviet Union as means of achieving legal recognition of 1945 borders of Poland and existence of East Germany. When the West agrees to these guarantees, Soviets agree in return to a "basket" of human rights provisions. Review of these provisions becomes duty of Commission on Security and Cooperation in Europe (CSCE), an organization that still meets to assess human rights issues.

1976

Riots over food prices in Poland. After Gierek's government puts them down with violence, intellectuals form Workers' Defense Committee (KOR), initiating cooperation between workers and intellectuals in Polish opposition.

1977

Czech intellectuals issue a charter calling on Czechoslovakia to respect human rights agreements it has signed. "Charter 77 is not an organization; it has no rules, permanent bodies, or formal membership. It embraces everyone who agrees with its ideas." This anti-political group turns away from trying to reform socialism and begins what Václav Havel calls "living in truth." Similar movements in other Eastern Bloc countries undermine moral legitimacy of socialist regimes.

1979

June

Pope John Paul II visits his native country, Poland, creating a "psychological earthquake." Citizens see it is possible to speak publicly of human life in terms other than stilted Communist rhetoric.

December

Soviet Union invades Afghanistan.

August 1980–December 1981

Gierek's new agenda failing in Poland. Measures to elevate Poland's standard of living increase foreign debt, but not productivity. This leads to economic problems and higher prices. Strikes begin to spread. Workers in Gdańsk shipyard set up inter-factory strike committee under leadership of Lech Wałesa. Government negotiates, finally agrees to creation of independent trade union, Solidarity. For sixteen months government and Solidarity struggle over union's role in society. Gaining ten million members almost overnight, Solidarity becomes for Polish society a beacon of hope for better life. Government makes limited concessions. General Wojciech Jaruzelski declares martial law in December 1981, imprisoning Solidarity leadership and banning union. Policy of "normalization" begins under direction of Jaruzelski's Military Council for National Salvation (WRON).

1982

In the Soviet Union, Brezhnev dies and is succeeded by Yuri Andropov, who dies in 1984. He is replaced by ailing Konstantin Chernenko.

1985

Chernenko dies. Mikhail Gorbachev assumes leadership of Soviet Union. Very quickly he sets out his "new thinking," which embraces *perestroika* (restructuring the economy) and *glasnost* (more openness in society). Pundits question just how far reforms will go.

1986

April

Soviet nuclear reactor in Chernobyl explodes and releases radiation throughout western Soviet Union and Europe.

December 16

Gorbachev allows Andrei Sakharov, famous physicist and dissident, to return to Moscow from six years' exile in Gorky.

1986–87

In Poland, Jaruzelski's dual policy of repressing Solidarity while at the same time taking measures to make public life more inclusive seems to be bearing fruit. Post-1981 Solidarity underground creates phenomenal variety of clandestine publications. Economic problems persist.

May 28, 1987

Nineteen-year-old West German Mathias Rust flies across eight hundred miles of restricted Soviet air space and lands his small plane in Red Square. Gorbachev sacks responsible generals.

December 1987

Pursuing active policy to lessen tensions with West, Gorbachev joins United States in signing IMF treaty banning intermediate range nuclear missiles. Earlier in the year he visits Prague and Bucharest, hinting broadly that Soviet Bloc countries should introduce *perestroika* and *glasnost*. Cool receptions by Husák and Nicolae Ceauşescu, increasingly megalomaniac Romanian dictator.

1987–88

Hungary's party reformers challenge leadership of János Kádár. Hungary started economic reform in 1968, authorizing "alternative forms of ownership," and by early 1980s had legalized a "second economy" and formed limited economic ties with West. Hungarians begin to experience forms of economic activity other than centralized economy. Democratic opposition finds issues that mobilize popular opinion, such as the 1956 Hungarian Revolution, the death of Imre Nagy, and the environment. Party reformers call for introduction of market mechanisms. The opposition calls for a "New Social Contract" featuring separation of powers.

November 29, 1987

Jaruzelski conducts referendum asking Poles if they are willing to make sacrifices for economic reforms. Answer: no, at least not if reforms are linked to the Jaruzelski government.

1988

February-March

Serious ethnic violence in Soviet republics of Armenia and Azerbaijan. Soviet troops intervene, thirty-one killed at Sumgait, Azerbaijan.

May

Lengthy struggle by Hungarian reform Communists, who realize need for further economic reform, results in Kádár's removal as Hungarian leader. Public sympathy for opposition demonstrations increases, especially those honoring Nagy, martyr of the 1956 revolution, but government refuses to reinterpret uprising in anti-Soviet way.

Soviet troops begin to withdraw from Afghanistan.

Strikes in Poland led by young workers not sympathetic to "old timers" in Solidarity.

Estonia and Lithuania declare themselves sovereign; Latvia follows suit on July 29.

June-July

Gorbachev conducts Soviet party conference with open debate televised to the public. Decision to hold free election for Supreme Soviet in 1989.

August

New round of strikes in Poland, this time organized by Solidarity with Lech Wałesa as leader, recalling spectre of 1980-81. New government under leadership of Rakowski, a Communist leader, initially agrees to hold "roundtable discussions" with Solidarity, then stalls discussion process. Discouragement.

October

Boris Yeltsin dropped from Soviet party leadership after he criticizes Gorbachev and the slow pace of Soviet reforms.

December

Gorbachev speech at United Nations pledges troop reductions and withdrawals, and stresses that "freedom of choice is a universal principle" that applies to both "the capitalist and the socialist systems."

1989

January

Jaruzelski forces Polish party to stop stalling and begin roundtable discussions with Solidarity and Catholic Church. Wałesa and General Czesław Kiszczak are chief negotiators.

Hungarian parliament passes law on right of free association. "The modernization of Hungarian society cannot develop in the framework of an authoritarian political system," the edict states. Leadership, reluctantly accepting transition to pluralism, is challenged by reform Communists who want party to become like West European social democrats. Hungarian borders opened.

March

Free elections in the Soviet Union; many party stalwarts defeated.

Mass demonstration in Budapest celebrates Hungarian revolution of 1848. Communist "old guard" agrees to exhume and rebury Imre Nagy.

Roundtable agreement signed in Poland. Solidarity legalized; elections scheduled for June 1989. Agreement stipulates that Communists and allies will receive 65% of seats in lower house; others, including the Senate, openly contested. Fully free elections envisioned for 1994.

April 25

First Soviet troops leave Hungary.

May 2

Hungarian border guards dismantle border barriers—literally cutting down the "iron curtain."

June 4

Solidarity surprises even itself by winning all but one contested seat in Polish election. Major Communist party leaders are defeated though running unopposed (more than half the voters cross their names off the ballot).

June 16

Massive public ceremony in Budapest marks reburial of Imre Nagy.

June 23

Roundtable discussions between party and opposition begin in Hungary, resulting in a new constitution and election laws. Opposition splits over method of electing president and whether it will favor Communists. Referendum is called.

June-July

Bulgaria expels 300,000 citizens of Turkish origin. Harbinger of ethnic problems throughout the Balkans.

July 6

Gorbachev speaks to Council of Europe in Strasbourg, France, emphasizing "our common European home." At Warsaw Pact meeting the next day he reiterates his pledge not to interfere in the affairs of Central and East European nations.

August

East German vacationers in Hungary start to cross border to Austria en route to West Germany at rate of several hundred a day. Others seek refuge in West German embassies in Prague and elsewhere.

August 24

In Poland, it becomes clear that Solidarity can put together the votes to elect its own government, and Jaruzelski, who the Solidarity leadership has already permitted to become president, agrees. On this date an emotional ceremony makes Tadeusz Mazowiecki, Catholic Solidarity editor and activist, the first non-Communist prime minister of a Soviet Bloc country in forty years.

September 1

Hungary abrogates agreement with East Germany whereby exit to West through Hungary is illegal.

September 11

More than 10,000 East Germans cross Austria from Hungary to West Germany. Erich Honecker, leader of East Germany since 1971, refuses to acknowledge crisis. Monday night prayer meetings for peace begin in Leipzig.

October 5

Seven thousand East Germans leave West German embassy in Prague and travel by train through East Germany, where they are "expelled" to West Germany. Riots ensue when still more people try to jump on trains.

Imre Nagy, leader of the 1956 Hungarian Revolt, is reburied with honors, June 16, 1989. Photo by László Haris.

Funeral for victims of attack by Soviet armed forces, Vilnius, Lithuania, Jan. 1991. Photo by Alvydas Lukys.

October 5-7

Gorbachev arrives in East Germany for strained celebrations marking the country's fortieth anniversary; tells leader Honecker "Life punishes those who delay." East German police put down anti-Honecker demonstrators.

October 9

Fifty thousand march in Leipzig. Government decision not to use force to clear streets gives green light for demonstrations in East Germany. By month's end, demonstrations of several hundred thousand occur in Leipzig and elsewhere.

October 18

East German party drops Honecker in desperate ploy to survive. Honecker protege, Egon Kranz, assumes leadership.

October 27

Warsaw Pact reaffirms that no member has right to interfere in political affairs of another.

November 4

Half a million persons protest the new government in East Berlin.

November 9

In attempting to report a decision to revise travel regulations, East German press spokesman implies border crossings may be made freely. Within minutes people show up at Berlin Wall and, after some hesitation, are let through.

By midnight hundreds of thousands of cheering people pass though, climbing on the Wall, popping champagne corks. The Wall has fallen.

November 10

Todor Zhivkov, Bulgarian president since 1954, forced to resign by reform Communists. Government promises free elections, to reject monopoly of power. Opposition immediately forms United Democratic Front and pluralist politics begin.

November 17

During an officially sanctioned demonstration in Prague, police attempt to block students' access to Wenceslas Square. Two students killed, many others beaten. Nine straight nights of increasingly large gatherings in the square follow.

November 21

Václav Havel, dissident playwright imprisoned earlier in the year by the Czech regime, addresses Prague rally of 200,000 and announces that the newly formed Civic Forum has begun negotiations with government.

November 25

Hundreds of thousands hear Havel and Alexander Dubček, reform leader of 1968, speak in Prague.

November 27

General strike in Czechoslovakia.

November 29

Hungarians narrowly approve referendum to postpone presidential election, thus ruining chances of Imre Poszgay, leading Communist reformer, to become president. Overwhelming vote to ban Workers' Guards, the armed party unit in every factory.

December 3

Entire East German politburo, including Krenz, resigns. One week later new leader selected with implicit mission to oversee demise of Communist party.

December 4

Warsaw Pact formally admits that the 1968 invasion of Czechoslovakia was a mistake.

December 15

Decision to relocate dissident Hungarian pastor sparks riots in Timişoara, Romania. All ethnic groups join in.

December 17

Ceauşescu, who had been in power since 1965 and had ruined his country's economy and brutalized his people, orders his generals to put down Timişoara's "hooligans and outside agitators" by force. Many are killed. Ceauşescu leaves for routine visit to Iran. Clashes with police spread throughout Romania.

December 21

Ceauşescu addresses crowd in Bucharest. Usually such occasions were minutely choreographed to ensure satisfactory results, but not this time. A national TV audience watches Ceauşescu look up in astonishment and wave his hands ineffectually when jeers and cries of "Ceauşescu dictator" arise from the crowd.

December 22

Ceauşescu "escapes" by helicopter, but is captured. National Salvation Front announces itself provisional government. Brief but violent confrontations in Bucharest. The National Library is destroyed by fire.

December 25

Ceauşescu and wife Elena tried by military "kangaroo court" and executed.

December 29

Havel is elected president of Czechoslovakia, and Dubček becomes head of Federal Assembly through an agreement worked out during month of December between the government, the Communist party, and Civic Forum.

1990

January 1

Havel addresses the Czechoslovak nation: "People, your government has returned to you!"

Solidarity government in Poland begins economic "shock therapy."

January 22

League of Yugoslav Communists party meeting breaks up in disarray. Slovenia and Croatia decide to hold democratic elections.

February–March

Local elections in Soviet Union bring reformers to power in Moscow and Leningrad. Many party stalwarts defeated.

March 11

Lithuania declares its independence.

March 18

Elections in East Germany won by Christian Democrats, with support from Helmut Kohl and West German party members. The rapid unification of Germany is their campaign platform.

March

Romania: violence in Transylvania between Hungarians and Romanians raises questions about future stability of region.

April

Hungarians elect conservative democratic government led by Hungarian Democratic Forum (MDF). Party system emerging.

May 20

In Romania, National Salvation Front, led by retreaded Communists, wins a questionable election. A few weeks later, the newly elected government transports miners into Bucharest to put down student protesters and opposition.

May 29

Boris Yeltsin elected head of Russian Republic.

June 17

Bulgaria elects new government. Ex-Communists win majority vote, but United Democratic Front attains presidency and substantial role as opposition party.

July 1

East Germany enters into monetary and trade union with West Germany, resulting in sudden bankruptcy of many East German firms. As Soviet economy weakens, trade opportunities disappear in Central and Eastern European countries.

July 16

Ukraine declares its sovereignty, followed by several other Soviet republics.

September 12

United States, France, Britain, and Soviet Union, the four occupying powers after World War II, sign agreement recognizing reunification of Germany.

October 3

Germany is reunited.

October 9

Supreme Soviet grants equal status to all political parties, ending exclusive legal status of Communist party in the workplace.

December 9

Lech Wałesa wins election as Polish president.

December

Successful economic reforms of Yugoslav central government collapse in face of resistance from the six republics. Yugoslav republic of Slovenia says it will declare indepen-

Untitled

Margua Haavamägi, Estonia, 1986

Haavamägi protests the manufacture of atomic weapons on the Baltic Coast, suggesting it should instead be a peace zone.

dence the next June. Croatia follows suit. Serbia says it will support the Serbian minority in Croatia if Croatia declares independence.

December 20

Eduard Shevardnadze, Soviet foreign minister and close Gorbachev ally, resigns suddenly, warns "a dictatorship is approaching."

1991

January

Czechoslovakia's Civic Forum splits into two parties. Process of pluralization continues in all Central and Eastern European countries to varying degrees. Serious economic difficulties.

Intervention by Soviet forces stirs unrest in Baltic states. Fifteen protestors killed in Lithuania; Latvian ministry of interior stormed.

February

Warsaw Pact dissolved. Council for Mutual Economic Assistance collapses.

February-March

Pro-democracy demonstrations in Albania lead to free elections and new government.

June

Croatia and Slovenia declare independence; federal Yugoslav forces invade Slovenia but withdraw shortly thereafter. Escalating tensions in July and August lead to civil war in Croatia as the Serbs and federal army battle the Croats. European Community attempts mediation with limited success.

July

Bulgarians approve new democratic constitution.

August

Conservative clique stages coup in Soviet Union, deposing Gorbachev. Boris Yeltsin leads resistance, and coup collapses within three days from popular pressure. Outpouring of anti-Communist emotion in Soviet Union. Gorbachev returns to Moscow, within days starts process of political transformation.

September 5

Supreme Soviet dissolves itself, seeks to establish new links among republics.

September 6

Independence of Baltic states recognized by Soviet Union and international community.

Author's note:
As this timeline is completed in September 1991, analysts are only beginning to interpret the events of 1989-91. As far as the future of the nations of Central and Eastern Europe is concerned, the only certainty is that surprises await us.

INDEX OF WRITERS AND ARTISTS

PERMISSIONS

Our gratitude is extended to the authors and publishers for permission to reprint the following materials:

"Berlin: Wall's End" from *The Magic Lantern* by Timothy Garton Ash. Copyright ©1990 by Timothy Garton Ash. First appeared in *The New York Review of Books,* January 19, 1990. Reprinted by permission of Random House, Inc.

Excerpt from *Comrade Agressor* by Jindřich Marco. Copyright ©1968 by Jindřich Marco. Reprinted by permission of the author.

"A Conversation with Mircea Dinescu" from *Romanian Notes* by Michael March. Copyright ©1991 by Michael March. By permission of the author.

"A Feast of Free Souls" by Lyubomir Nikolov. Copyright ©1991 by Lyubomir Nikolov. By permission of the author.

"Keeping Calm in Prague" by George Konrád. First appeared in *The Guardian,* in April 1990. Copyright ©1990 by George Konrád. Reprinted by permission of the author and *The Guardian.*

Excerpt from *November Hurricane* by Bohumil Hrabal. Copyright ©1990 by Bohumil Hrabal. Reprinted by permission of the author.

"One Hundred Meters of Democracy" by Inna and Sergei Pichuginy, Sergei Oskolkov, Vladimir Ivanov. Copyright ©1988 by the authors. Reprinted by permisssion of the editor of *Rodnik* and the authors.

"Renaming the Past" by Zinovy Zinik. Copyright ©1991 by Zinovy Zinik. Reprinted by permission of the author.

"Report from a Besieged City" by Zbigniew Herbert. First appeared in *The New York Review of Books,* August 1983, translated by Czesław Miłosz. Copyright ©1982 by Zbigniew Herbert. Reprinted by permission of the author.

"The State of the Empire" by Ivan Klíma. First appeared in *Granta* 30, 1990. Copyright ©1990 by Ivan Klíma. Reprinted by permission of the author and *Granta.*

"Contention and Friction" by Miroslav Holub. Copyright ©1991 by Miroslav Holub. Reprinted by permission of the author.

"The Transition" by Péter Esterházy. Copyright ©1990 by Péter Esterházy. By permission of the author.

"A Warsaw Diary, 1983" by Ryszard Kapuściński. First appeared in *Granta* 15 & 16, 1985. Copyright ©1985 by Ryszard Kapuściński. Reprinted by permission of the author and *Granta.*

"For Peter Weiss" by Steffen Mensching; "More Notes on the Theme of Changing Places" by Lutz Rathenow; "Poems on Maps" by Viktor Krivulin; "Scrap" and "Hat" by Tomasz Jastrun; "Standard Isolation" by Ion Morar; "Theology of Hopelessness" and "Stalin" by Vladimir Levchev; "They Will Have Eyes to See" by Juris Kunnoss; "You Have Built Me a House" by Wolfgang Hilbig reprinted from *Child of Europe: A New Anthology of East European Poetry.* Copyright ©1990 by Michael March. Reprinted by permission of Michael March and Penguin Books Ltd.

THIS BOOK is a coproduction of the Smithsonian Institution Traveling Exhibition Service and Universe Publishing, New York. The editing and design of this book was supervised by the publications department, SITES. Publications Director, Andrea Stevens. The book was edited by Melissa Hirsch. Copyeditors, editorial consultants, and editorial support staff for this project include Elizabeth Kennedy, Sally Hoffmann, David Andrews, Lindsey Adams, Cynthia Haley, and Stephanie Fullen. Translators include Richard Aczel and András Fürész (Hungarian); Dorota Adams, Daniel Bourne, Adam Czerniawski, Edward Michaels, and Czesław Miłosz (Polish); Bissy Genova and Ewald Osers (Bulgarian); Geraldine Cavalier-Holubová, Rudolf Fischer, Dáša Helmick, Dana Hábová, Stanislav Kolář, Edward Michaels, Marie Vaňková, and David Young (Czech); Elizabeth Jezierski (Russian); Oana Lungescu (Romanian); Michael March and Dušan Puvačić (Serbo-Croatian); Richard McKane and Michael Molnar (Russian, Latvian); Agnes Stein and Paul Tesar (German). The posters were photographed by the Smithsonian's Office of Printing and Photographic Services: Richard Strauss, Richard Hofmeister, Joe Goulait, and Terry McCrae. The production of this book was supervised by Adele Ursone, editorial director, Universe Publishing, with assistance from Gladys Garcia and James Stave. Electronic composition in Adobe Garamond and Frutiger. Printing and bindery by Kim Hup Lee, Singapore. Interior typography and layout by Polly Sexton Graphic Design, Washington, DC. Book concept and cover art designed by Dana Bartelt, Raleigh, NC.